Max Weber and Karl Marx

Karl Löwith, with a new preface by
Bryan S. Turner

Edited and with an Introduction by
Tom Bottomore and William Outhwaite

London and New York

First published 1993
by Routledge
11 New Fetter Lane, London EC4P 4EE

Simultaneously published in the USA and Canada
by Routledge
29 West 35th Street, New York, NY 10001

Phototypeset in Palatino by Intype, London
Printed and bound in Great Britain by
Biddles Ltd, Guildford and King's Lynn

British Library Cataloguing in Publication Data
A catalogue record for this book is available from the
British Library.

Library of Congress Cataloging in Publication Data
Löwith, Karl, 1897–1973.
  [Max Weber und Karl Marx. English]
  Max Weber and Karl Marx/Karl Löwith, with a new
preface by Bryan S. Turner.
      p.   cm. – (Routledge classics in sociology)
  Includes bibliographical references and index.
  1. Weber, Max, 1864–1920. 2. Marx, Karl, 1818–1883.
3. Sociology–Germany–History. I. Title. II. Series:
Routledge sociology classics.
HM22.G3W4545313   1993
301'.092'2–dc20   93–18705
                                          CIP

ISBN 0–415–09381–3

Contents

Preface to the new edition of Karl Löwith's *Max Weber and Karl Marx*[1]

Bryan S. Turner

Modern man has forgotten to listen to this silence. Our
world becomes increasingly loud, noisy – deafening with
noise. We can no longer hear and our words have become
false.

Karl Löwith

INTRODUCTION

Sociology has, since its institutional foundation in the late nineteenth century, been subject to profound changes in paradigms
and perspectives. Many of these conceptual revolutions have
challenged the fundamental assumptions of their discipline by,
for example, bringing into question the whole idea of 'the
social' (Baudrillard 1983). While the history of all academic
disciplines can be written in terms of violent paradigmatic shifts
(Kuhn 1970), sociology appears more prone than most subjects
to bewildering shifts in intellectual terrain. One can either
regard this analytical instability in a negative fashion as indicating the lack of maturity of sociology as a social science, or one
can see sociology as a disciplinary field which is acutely in tune
with the broad sweep of cultural movements within modern
societies. The swings and changes in analytical paradigms are
thus a response to broader societal currents.

However, within this context of intellectual uncertainty, one
relatively persistent dimension of sociology has been its unre-
solved and critical relationship to the legacy of Karl Marx. More
precisely, the debate over the relationship between Marx's
political economy and Max Weber's interpretative sociology,
which has raged with varying degrees of intensity since the

publication of *The Protestant Ethic and the Spirit of Capitalism* (Weber 1932) in 1904, has determined many of the major issues for research in the social sciences in the twentieth century.

These controversies have been driven by many forces, both scientific and ideological. For example, the sociological curriculum has been transformed in the post-war period by feminism, to a lesser extent by ethnic politics such as the black movement and more recently by ecological debates. Over a longer period, it has been coloured by the changing political fortunes of both Marxism as a social movement and by sociology as an academic discipline. Part of the hostility between Marxists and academic sociologists is a function of their family resemblance; they both subscribe to grand theories of the historical development of society and both claim to offer a scientific analysis of those conditions which will bring about revolutionary changes in social structure. They are pre-eminently explanations of the nature of modern societies, of which the capitalist economy is a central feature. Marxism and sociology have, however, typically adhered to profoundly different epistemologies, philosophies and presuppositions.

Although they can be distinguished in these terms, the fortunes of Marxism, socialism and sociology, especially in Western Europe, have often been closely interrelated. Classical sociology at various points in its development was forced to confront socialism as a social fact and socialism as a competing theory of society. For example, Saint-Simon was simultaneously the founder of French socialism and sociology. Both Durkheim and Weber wrote extensively on the nature of socialism and Marxism. Durkheim in particular adopted a sympathetic approach to socialism as a moral regulation of the economy which would restrain the anomic effects of utilitarian ideology and market conflicts (Durkheim 1958). Weber was highly critical of the rationalisation of economic life which a centralised socialist economic plan would entail, but he was also significantly influenced in his view of the economic structure of the ancient civilisations by Marx's theory of slavery and feudalism (Weber 1976). Weber also once claimed that the intellectual seriousness of scholars was to be judged by their attitude towards Nietzsche and Marx; Weber's own inaugural address at Freiburg University in 1895 was peppered with references and asides to Nietzsche's views on the will to power and to

Marx's economic analyses (Tribe 1989). Joseph Schumpeter, who was professionally an economist, contributed to the creation of economic sociology, but regarded the socialisation of economic functions as a corrosion of entrepreneurial creativity (Schumpeter 1934). Alternatively, sociological theorists have often been criticised precisely for their failure to take Marxism as a theory of society seriously. Thus, Talcott Parsons has been challenged because he treated Marxism as simply a version of utilitarian economic theory and therefore as an analysis of society that is consequently flawed by its narrow positivist assumptions (Gould 1991). In fact, in Europe, sociology has often been inadequately represented in the academy as a consequence of its association with radical social movements.

While this intellectual and political relationship has been variable between different authors and sociological traditions, as a general rule, one can argue that Marxism and sociology have been typically opposed to each other, because they have in part been competing for a similar intellectual audience. Marxists have been critical of academic sociology since at least the 1930s when they objected to writers such as Karl Mannheim who had developed a relativising sociology of knowledge that challenged Marxist approaches to ideology (Mannheim 1991). By contrast, Marxist authors like Georg Lukács saw sociology as the manifestation of bourgeois irrationalism (Lukács 1971). According to the 'official' view of Marxism and sociology, the whole orientation of Marxism has been towards a committed critique of capitalism as a system of unjust exploitation, whereas Weberian sociology, with its individualistic approach to methodology and its separation of facts and values, has been either overtly neutral in political terms or covertly an aspect of liberal social philosophy.

This intellectual struggle between academic sociology and Marxist political economy to dominate the character of sociology was probably at its height from the 1960s to the late 1970s, when various manifestations of French social theory, such as structuralism, were at the foreground of intellectual development. Louis Althusser (Althusser and Balibar 1968) adopted the idea of an 'epistemological rupture' from philosophers of science such as Gaston Bachelard to argue that Marxism was a science of the transformation of modes of production, which avoided the common-sense or subjective notions of sociology. This Althusserian structuralism was adopted by writers like Nicos Poulantzas (1973) to claim that sociology, by concentrating on the attitudes and experiences of individuals, could not provide a scientific analysis of the determining structures of economics and politics. This analytical contrast between the structuralism of scientific Marxism and the methodological individualism of 'bourgeois sociology' dominated much of the theoretical development of the social sciences in the 1970s. In sociology, the theoretical contrast was often presented in terms of Weber's methodological individualism and commitment to sociology as an interpretative perspective on social action, on the one hand, and Marx's realist epistemology, structuralism and commitment to historical materialism as a science of modes of production on the other (Hindess and Hirst 1975). These debates, which were also reflections of broader political struggles in Western societies, largely ignored Weber's historical analyses of the role of 'objective interests' in politics and economics, and his preoccupations with the negative unintended consequences of action (Turner 1981). At the same time, Althusser was forced to argue that the 'early Marx' of the Paris Manuscripts was trapped in a humanistic paradigm which was eventually abandoned in favour of the scientific approach of *Capital*, Volume one (Althusser 1966). The consequence was a largely sterile debate about the character of orthodox Marxism: was the early Marx's humanism compatible with the deterministic understanding of Marxist Leninism by the Party?

One must also add that this intellectual contest was far more important in Europe than in North America, partly because socialism as a political force has never had much significance in American politics (Lipsett 1960). American sociology produced a number of radical sociologists such as C. Wright Mills and Alvin Gouldner, but they were somewhat marginal to the mainstream of American sociology in the 1950s and 1960s, which remained liberal and reformist in politics, and empirical and applied in its scientific orientation. Many of the American sociologists who fell outside the applied tradition of mainstream American sociology were in fact either European exiles (such as Hans Gerth and Leo Lowenthal) or Canadians (such as Dennis Wrong).

The relationship between sociology and Marxism has in the

last two decades gone through many phases, but basically the whole issue of sociology versus Marxism has in recent times been transformed by three interrelated changes: the dramatic political collapse of organised communism in 1989–90, which has inevitably brought into question the intellectual credibility of Marxism as a critical theory of society and history; the rapid re-establishment of sociology in the academies of the re-constituted east European universities in the 1990s, especially in Germany, Hungary and Poland; and the widespread interest in postmodernism as an alternative to the 'grand narratives' of humanism, the Enlightenment and Marxism (Turner 1990). These socio-political changes have been significant for both sociology and Marxism, but it is obviously the case that there is a more general crisis of intellectual authority and direction in Marxism as a theory of society than in sociology.

Of course, Marxist intellectuals have often taken the view that organised communism either had no necessary relation-ship to Marxism as a theory of society, or that the Marxism of Karl Marx is still the most effective general criticism of the exploitation of workers in capitalism and of the authoritarian regimes of Soviet-style state socialism. In reality, the authority of Marxist theory has been severely challenged, not least for the failure of Marxism to anticipate the total collapse of east European communism and the Soviet Union. To argue that the collapse of organised communism as a political force and the destruction of state socialism as a form of society have no bearing on the intellectual credibility of Marxism would be rather like arguing that the discovery of the bones of Christ in an Israeli grave-yard, the abdication of the Pope, and the clos-ure of Christendom would have no relevance to the intellectual coherence of Christian theology. Radical thinkers like Ernesto Laclau are surely correct in arguing that socialist thought cannot simply turn its back on the history of 'actually existing Marxism'. Marxist theory has to be re-constituted from the foundations upwards and this re-constitution will necessarily involve a fundamental re-appraisal of the scientific and political relationship between Marxism and sociology, that is between Marx and Weber.

LÖWITH'S HEIDEGGERIAN EXISTENTIALISM

This convoluted and protracted debate explains the continuing interest in and importance of Karl Löwith's study of Weber and Marx which was published in Germany in 1932 in the *Archiv für Sozialwissenschaft und Sozialpolitik*, and was subsequently translated into English in 1982. Löwith wrote and worked in an academic and political context in Germany where Marxism and sociology were polarised. Weber's sociology of religion was welcomed by many German social scientists as the definitive answer to Marxist theories of ideology. With the rise of fascism in Germany in the 1930s, Marxism was of course very much under attack, but sociology was also regarded with some suspicion because it was itself associated with the Jewish intellectual community, which included such figures as Georg Simmel, Karl Mannheim and Norbert Elias. However, recent research on the history of German sociology under National Socialism has demonstrated that sociology was not an oppositional force and largely acquiesced in the reactionary university culture of the Nazi period (Turner and Kassler 1992). By contrast, the members of the Institute of Social Research (the so-called Frankfurt School), which was initially inspired by Marxism, fled to the United States, where they lived as reluctant exiles (Jay 1973). Löwith's study of Weber and Marx was thus published in a context of political instability, where scholarship was increasingly politicised. As we will see, Löwith's own work and life were bound up intellectually with the theory of history, the legacy of Hegelian idealism and Marxism, and bound up politically with the impact of fascism on Jewish intellectuals in Germany.

Löwith's study of Weber and Marx is now sixty years old, but it is crucially important for three basic reasons. First, Löwith was able to show that, despite the very important differences between Marx and Weber, their sociological perspectives were held together by a convergent philosophical anthropology. Thus, while the political attitudes of Marx and Weber were diametrically opposed, they shared a fundamental interest in the problem of 'man'[2] in bourgeois capitalism. There was therefore an important convergence in their attitudes towards the negative features of bourgeois civilisation, which Marx elaborated through the idea of 'alienation' and Weber through the idea of 'rationalisation'. For both authors, capitalist society was, from their relatively similar views on ontology, inescapably problematic, but also revolutionary by comparison with the traditional civilisations of both the Western world and Asia. Capitalism, which brought about a profound 'de-traditionalisation' of society (Beck 1992) created enormous risks for humans, but also opened up new transformative opportunities. For Marx, the opportunity for social transformation was to be seized ultimately by the revolutionary struggles of the working class. For Weber, the transformative potential was an essential feature of capitalist modernisation, but he was ambiguous about any ultimate escape from 'the iron cage'. In this sense, Weber's sociology was fatalistic, because it concentrated on the negative and unintended aspects of social action (Turner 1981). Weber's sociology was driven by a concern for 'human dignity' (Löwith 1982: 22), but Weber remained pessimistic about the opportunities for human freedom within a society which had been so thoroughly subjected to the processes of rationalisation. This difference in their attitudes was neatly expressed by Löwith, namely 'Marx proposes a therapy while Weber has only a "diagnosis" to offer' (Löwith 1982: 25).

Thus the first important feature of Löwith's general interpretation of Marx and Weber was that, by concentrating attention on 'this underlying anthropological concern' (Löwith 1982: 20), Löwith was able to show that the differences between Marx and Weber in terms of their epistemological, scientific and political views were actually grounded in a similar philosophical anthropology. It is important to keep in mind that Löwith's thesis that there was a similar and crucial underlying philosophical anthropology in Marxism and Weberian sociology was published in 1932, many decades before recent interpretations which have presented similar arguments, for example about the impact of Nietzsche on Weber (Hennis 1987). Löwith's work was highly original and anticipated many contemporary studies which have also focused on the underlying ontological assumptions of the social theories of Marx and Weber. Although a number of writers in the Marxist tradition have analysed the philosophical anthropology in Marx's early work such as *The Economic and Philosophical Manuscripts of 1844* (Marx 1964), the implicit understanding of 'man' in Weber continues to be neglected, with the possible exception of Wilhelm Hennis.

Löwith's perspective on Weber provides an essential starting point for uncovering this hidden ontology in Weber's post-Christian analysis of human beings and their striving to achieve 'personality'.

Löwith's thesis continues to be important, secondly, because it was developed out of his philosophical indebtedness to Martin Heidegger. I shall show shortly that Heidegger was primarily concerned to understand the nature of Being, but Heidegger wanted to avoid the abstraction of traditional metaphysics which started with universal observations about Being. In *Being and Time* (Heidegger 1962) which appeared in German in 1927, Heidegger rejected metaphysics by concentrating on the contingent facticity of being in the everyday world. Being or *Da-sein* was always 'being-there' in time and space. However, human beings were constantly in danger of forgetting their place in this everyday world of being. Human beings are to some extent always homeless beings; being without a place in the world, they are alienated from their reality. They are ontologically nostalgic (Turner 1987) in this condition of existential homelessness (*Heimatlosigkeit*). Heidegger went on to develop a critique of technology in capitalist society (Heidegger 1977) because it created conditions in which human beings are increasingly alienated from their own bodies. Heidegger, who was particularly interested in the importance of the human hand, refused apparently to use a typewriter, because it was a further alienation of mind and body (Derrida 1989). Löwith as a student of Heidegger was of course profoundly influenced by this analysis of existence (Löwith 1948) and the Heideggerian contribution to existentialism.[3] For Löwith, the Heideggerian analysis of the classical problem of essence and existence was the starting point of modern philosophy and hence the starting point for an adequate philosophical understanding of Marx and Weber. It was this Heideggerian dimension to Löwith's approach which made Löwith's analysis highly original and enduring. Heidegger's analysis of Being has been crucial to many developments in twentieth-century philosophy, such as phenomenology and existentialism, but it has also been increasingly important in post-structuralism and postmodernism. For example, Heidegger's hostility to traditional metaphysics, his close concentration on the etymology of basic concepts in philosophical analysis and the textuality of his philosophical method have been important in the development of so-called deconstructive techniques in modern philosophy, especially in the contributions of Jacques Derrida. Löwith's study of Weber and Marx from the perspective of Heideggerian existentialism has retained a freshness and relevance to modern philosophical discussion which should not be ignored.[4]

Thirdly, Heidegger's approach to the critique of metaphysics was in its turn shaped by Nietzsche's critique of conventional metaphysics, his hostility to traditional religious values and his commitment to the creation of a 're-valuation of values' which would overcome the mediocrity of the moral life of 'the herd' in modern society. Nietzsche's prophetic slogan that 'God is dead' was the starting point of modern philosophy which has been structured by the question which was central to Nietzsche's philosophy: what are the moral and social consequences of the death of God, that is the termination of a view of reality in which a personal god still made sense? The collapse of the certainties of the traditional view of reality had left an enormous chasm and Löwith interprets the development of modern philosophy as, in large measure, a response to this absence of certainty. Of course, Löwith has been primarily concerned with the modern development of existentialism as a response to the post-Christian world. In particular, Nietzsche, Kierkegaard and Heidegger have been philosophers who concentrated on the contingent character of life and the pathos of the human condition. While Pascal could still draw some comfort from the regularities of the physical world, modern existentialists (from Kierkegaard to Sartre) have viewed nature 'only as the hidden background of man's forlorn existence' (Löwith 1952: 91). We might add that Weber's persistently bleak and negative view of the world (perhaps best summarised in his 'I want to see how much I can stand' announcement) was also part of this critical legacy. While Weber described himself as, in religious terms, 'unmusical', he was also deeply moved by the pathos of a post-Christian reality which had yet to produce an alternative world-view.

While Nietzsche was crucially important for the development of modern philosophy, it is only relatively recently that sociologists have recognised the importance of Nietzsche for sociology as a consequence of his impact on, for example, Weber, Simmel and Scheler (Stauth and Turner 1988). It is for example impossible to understand Simmel's ideas about the tragedy of culture and the nature of social forms without understanding Simmel's dependence on Schopenhauer and Nietzsche (Simmel 1991). Nietzsche is important for sociological theory because he formulated an analysis of cultural change which presents the problem of social cohesion in terms of an erosion of normative authority and politics. In short, Nietzsche developed an important understanding of the nature of ideology and the state. For Nietzsche the primitive form of ideology is idolatry. Having claimed that in modern civilisation God is dead, Nietzsche was aware that new idols would fill the space which was left by this dead God; in particular, 'the herd' was increasingly subject to the state, which was the new idol that would rob people of their freedom. We can see Weber's anxieties about the slavery of modern people within the bureaucratic machine of the modern state and about the possibilities of personal autonomy in a world which had been transformed by the processes of rationalisation. Weber went out of his way to use Nietzschean language in his Freiburg address of 1895 to comment on the importance of political struggle in economic life in which the quest for 'elbow room' was central to all political life. Löwith's Heideggerian interpretation of Weber and Marx was thus also important because it began the important task of uncovering the Nietzschean roots of Weber's pessimistic analysis of modern, rational society.

LÖWITH'S LIFE AND WORKS

Löwith was born in 1897 and died in 1973. His life was eventful. He was a student in Freiburg where he came under the influence of Husserl and Heidegger. Löwith described his student years in Freiburg as 'incomparably rich and fruitful' in his brief account of his 'curriculum vitae' (Löwith 1959). It was Heidegger who directed Löwith's *Habilitationsschrift* on *Das Individuum in der Rolle des Mitmenschen* (Löwith 1928). He had the status of *Dozent* lecturer at Marburg University prior to Hitler's climb to power in 1933. During these crisis years, he travelled to Italy, Japan and finally America in 1941, taking up positions at the Hartford Theological Seminary and the New School for Social Research in New York (1949–51). It was at Hartford Theological Seminary that Löwith wrote a number of influential

articles on the philosophy of history, Marxism and existentialism for *Social Research*. He returned to Germany to take up a
professorship of philosophy at Heidelberg University.

Löwith was thus starting his academic career in the context
of significant developments in German philosophical thought.
At the beginning of this century, 'the south-west school' of
German philosophy at Heidelberg and Freiburg was the intellectual cradle of phenomenology and existentialism (in the
work of Husserl and Heidegger), interpretative sociology (in
the writing of Weber) and a rebirth of dialectical materialism
(in the Marxism of Lukács). The writers who were influenced
by E. Lask and Husserl included Karl Jaspers, Georg Lukács
and Ernst Bloch. It was within this fountain of academic development in philosophy, history and sociology that Löwith's
intellectual interests were formed.

Löwith's academic publications are extensive, but they are
primarily journal articles. Some of his philosophical essays have
been collected in his *Nature, History and Existentialism and Other
Essays* (Löwith 1966). His collected bibliography was edited by
Klaus Stichweh in *Von Hegel zu Nietzsche* (Löwith 1986) and a
further version is to be found in Löwith's *Samtliche Schriften*
(Löwith 1981) which was edited by Klaus Stichweh and Marc
B. de Launay. Löwith's reputation, especially outside German
academic life, is based on three major texts, namely *Max Weber
and Karl Marx* (Löwith 1982) in 1932, *From Hegel to Nietzsche*
(Löwith 1964) in 1941, and *Meaning in History* (Löwith 1970).

He published a number of short autobiographical essays of
which the most interesting is *Mein Leben in Deutschland vor und
nach 1933* (Löwith 1986) which was written in Japan in 1939.
This text is important because it contains an account of
his meeting with Heidegger in 1936, and his reflections on
Heidegger's philosophy in the context of German fascism.
Löwith met Heidegger for the last time in 1936, when
Heidegger was giving some lectures at the German-Italian
Culture Institute. Löwith, Heidegger's student and now an
exile from Germany, was particularly distressed by the fact that
Heidegger wore the Party insignia on his lapel during a family
excursion to Frascati and Tusculum. Löwith remarked that
Heidegger 'wore it during his entire stay in Rome, and it had
obviously not occurred to him that the swastika was out of
place while spending the day with me' (Löwith 1988: 115).

Löwith's *Heidegger: Denker in dürftiger Zeit* (Löwith 1953) has yet to be translated.

Löwith's social theory was closely bound up with his intellectual engagement with Heidegger and hence with the problems of theological thought in the modern world. His constant concern with the problems of faith and scepticism (Löwith 1951) was a product of the sense of crisis in post-war Germany and intellectually a product of his study of Kierkegaard and Heidegger. The presuppositions behind *Max Weber and Karl Marx* were primarily theological, but they are derived from a theology which was in large measure post-Christian. Of course, Löwith's intellectual and personal relationship with Heidegger cannot be easily separated from Heidegger's problematic and controversial relationship with fascism. Heidegger's personal commitment to National Socialism cannot be seriously doubted (Farias 1987). What is at issue is whether there was some necessary or 'natural' relationship between Heidegger's philosophy of Being and his views on fascism (Wolin 1988).

In this respect, Löwith's perspective on this issue is intrinsically interesting, because he recognised an analytical relationship between Heidegger's existentialist analysis of *Da-sein* as involving an authentic capacity-for-Being which is specific to each individual and which is an expression of their particular historical circumstances. Each individual is faced with the possibility of choice and personal responsibility. In fact within the context of the unfolding of German history, there is a duty (*Mussen*) to take a personal responsibility for one's being. Löwith recognised some affinity between Carl Schmitt's 'decisionism' in political philosophy and Heidegger's existential notion of the 'throwness' of being. One might also suggest a parallel between this Heideggerian notion of existential responsibility and Weber's famous and influential notion of the ethic of responsibility, which Weber connected to the ideas of calling and personality. For Weber, the ethic of responsibility finds its most elevated expression in the callings or vocations of science and politics. It is an interesting coincidence that Weber's inaugural address for the chair of economics was also delivered at the University of Freiburg in 1895 in which Weber also alluded, in language which self-consciously borrowed from Nietzsche, to the need for strong political decision-making if Germany was to survive in a competitive international context.

However, there is also a relationship between Hitler's idea of destiny, the fate of the German nation and his own charismatic calling to leadership. The facticity of our being propels us to a choice in which we may experience an authentication of life. Hitler's choice is one illustration of these ideas, but Heidegger's own rectorship of the University of Freiburg is another. Heidegger expressed these ideas about the authenticity of being and history in his 'The Self-Affirmation of the German University', the famous *Rekoratsrede* of 1933. In his momentous decision to act as rector and to support the National Socialist cause within the University, Heidegger's philosophy was transformed into contemporary German reality, 'and thus for the first time the master's will to action finds suitable terrain and the formal outline of the existential categories receives decisive content' (Löwith 1988: 125).

LÖWITH AND THE MEANING OF HISTORY

It is important to emphasise Löwith's academic relationship to Heidegger in order to understand Löwith's intellectual development, but more importantly to grasp his approach to Marx and Weber. Löwith's social philosophy is based on the view that the decisive feature of Western culture is to be located in the break between the classical world-view in which there is no history but the harmonious repetition of the same and the Christian *Weltanschauung* in which the advent of Christ creates a teleological framework for reality. History now has a meaning, which is primarily the revelation of grace through the creation and fall of man, the advent, death and resurrection of Christ, the lives of the saints and the Church, and ultimately the creation of a Second Kingdom. Whereas the classical world recognised the existence of a perfectly organised cosmos that was rational, Christian theology saw reality in terms of a divine telos, but also recognised that the ways of God to humanity were often obscure. Indeed the Beatitudes, which for example appear to celebrate the frailty and humility of Christians, express irrational values from the perspective of Greek rationalism. Christian theology has thus typically seen the Christian gospel as an offence to a rational mind, because Christianity rests ultimately on faith and not upon reason.

This fundamental historical contrast, perhaps the original

quarrel between the ancients and the moderns, shaped Löwith's entire approach to modern social theory, in particular his approach to Marx and Weber. It was for example the basic theme of *Meaning in History* and it shaped his approach to Hegel and Nietzsche in his famous account of the 'revolutionary bridge in nineteenth-century German thought' (Löwith 1964). To take one illustration of his approach, Löwith thought that Nietzsche's problematic commitment to the doctrine of Eternal Recurrence was not an aberration but the core of Nietzsche's philosophy (Löwith 1945). It was Nietzsche's views on the problem of history and the doctrine of the Eternal Recurrence which were constitutive of his ultimately ambiguous approach to religion, the problems of values and classical Greece. Nietzsche rejected Christianity as a form of decadence – as a form of neurosis – but he also recognised the radical implications of Christian eschatology. He was also aware that the modern doctrine of progress (and possibly the Darwinistic version of the idea of progress) were secularised versions of the Christian view of history as a progression of the faithful to the Kingdom of God. For Nietzsche, the Eternal Recurrence and its prophet Dionysus is an important component in his attempt to bring about a transvaluation of values. The Eternal Recurrence is seen by Nietzsche as a 'yes-saying philosophy' of self-affirmation against the Christian doctrine of a unique creation. Yet, as Löwith points out, Nietzsche is a modern man, who found an unconditional acceptance of the classical world-view problematic. Thus Nietzsche's 'great effort to re-marry man's destiny to cosmic fate or to "translate man back into nature" as the original text could not but be frustrated' (Löwith 1945: 283). Nietzsche's argument is, as a consequence, inconsistent. Nietzsche wanted to assert that the Eternal Recurrence was an objective fact which could be proved by modern physics and mathematics, but frequently presented the doctrine as a moral perspective or subjective viewpoint. Nietzsche was committed to a version of individuality in which human beings have to triumph over the limitations of society and history. This individuality was expressed in the idea that the principal task of every human being is to become who they are. This Nietzschean version of individuality, which is essentially a modern view, could not be reconciled with the classical idea that the world is simply an eternal cycle of impersonal rep-

etition. In a world which threatens human beings by its aim-
lessness and lack of purpose, it is the nature of human beings
to will to power. For Nietzsche, human beings will always
prefer to will nothingness than not to will at all. The failure of
Nietzsche's doctrine of the Eternal Recurrence 'was not that he
revived the classical vision of the *kosmos* as an eternal recurrence of the same, but that he attempted to establish its truth
by his own creative will, under the title of a "will to power" '
(Löwith 1952: 92).

This general view of the philosophy of history provides the
context for Löwith's view of Marx. For Löwith, Marx's historical
materialism is a secularised version of the Christian teleology.
Despite the scientific vocabulary of the Marxist vision of history, Löwith treats Marx's philosophy of history as a global
vision which depends fundamentally on the Christian scheme
of eschatology, the doctrine of the Last Days and the Restoration of man to Grace. In Marxism, 'history' is located in
the long interval between the loss of communal innocence in
primitive communism and its restoration in the final transition
to communism. The vale of tears in the Marxist historical framework is occupied by the creation of private property, the division of labour, the organisation of a market by exchange
values, and the brutalisation of the working class by capitalists.
In short, history is to do with human alienation. This interpretation of Marxism has often been challenged by Marxists who
want to reject any association between Christianity and Marxism, but it is an association which is difficult to dispel. For
example, the young Lukács's view of history as a series of
revolutions, which has the effect of bringing about moral puri-
fication and redemption, had a definitely apocalyptic quality.
Lukács is also highly relevant in this context, since it was
Lukács's theory of alienation that combined Weber's theme of
rationalisation with a Marxist analysis of reification.[5]

Löwith identified the theme of alienation in Marx's social
theory as constitutive of Marx's entire project. For Löwith, the
theme of 'man's self-alienation in the early writings of Marx'
(Löwith 1954) was not merely an optional extra or a youthful
aberration relating to Marx's humanism, but in fact a perspective which integrates the early writings on the anthropological
conditon of 'man' and the later writings on economic processes.
Löwith takes a strong stand, therefore, on the integration and

integrity of Marx's work as a whole. Marx's starting point is a critique of bourgeois social reality which is defined principally in terms of the alienation of human beings from themselves. Thus, *Capital* 'is not simply a critique of political economy but a critique of the man of bourgeois society in terms of that society's economy' (Löwith 1954: 215). The 'man of bourgeois society' is characterised by the separation of the private world of individualised private property and morality and the public realm of dignity and reason. Marx explored this problem of self-alienation and externalisation through religion, the economy and the polity. In religious alienation, the natural powers of 'man' are transferred to the divine powers of God (Feuerbach 1957); economic alienation takes the form of commodification and, ideologically, as the fetishisation of commodities; political self-estrangement is constituted by the separation of state and society; its social expression in capitalism is the historical creation of an alienated proletariat. Löwith never departed from this perspective on Marxism in which Marx's political economy is founded on the existential problem of the human condition.

MAX WEBER AND KARL MARX

In this new preface to Löwith's classical study, I have already indicated why Löwith's account of Marx and Weber has remained an original and powerful contribution to the development of social theory: it was thoroughly grounded in a philosophical understanding of the central issue of modern philosophy, namely the relationship between essence and existence. Löwith approaches Marx's materialist theory as a radicalisation of Hegel's idealism: Marx's solution was to argue that in communism at the 'end' of history the individual essence of each human being is overcome and resolved (*Aufhebung*) in communal existence. This Heideggerian question concerning existence which Löwith poses in relation to Marx's materialism, provides the link between Marx's philosophical anthropology, Weber's post-Christian existentialism and the postmodern, deconstructive writings of Derrida and Vattimo.

It is not necessary to attempt to summarise the specific arguments of Löwith's *Max Weber and Karl Marx*. My aim is to pick out certain aspects of Löwith's account which relate to this 'anthropological concern'. This selective commentary provides the framework within which one can then ask the question: what is enduring in Löwith's social theology?

To start with an apparently trivial observation, it is interesting to note that this is a study of Weber and Marx, not Marx and Weber. In other words, we can read this as an interpretation of Marx through a prior and more fundamental study of Weber. One can imagine that Weber was politically not congenial to Löwith, given Weber's nationalism and authoritarian view of German politics (Mommsen 1989). Löwith appears to be uncomfortable with the harsh words of Weber's Freiburg lecture in which Weber, in reviewing the political failure of both the Prussian Junkers and the bourgeoisie, 'presented some unpalatable truths to his own class'. However, Weber was part of a circle of German intellectuals which was greatly exercised by the historical role of Protestantism in Western culture and by the general problem of Christianity in relation to the development of secular, bourgeois capitalism. Indeed, Weber's celebrated Protestant Ethic Thesis can be understood as a specific contribution to this theological debate in which some of the most important contributions came from elsewhere, such as from the theology of Ernst Troeltsch (1931). It is also clear that Löwith sympathises with Weber's epistemological critique of Marxism as a 'science', a critique which was to some extent compatible with Heidegger's own deconstructive techniques. Löwith's study has, therefore, to be read from the perspective of Weber's criticisms of Marxism as a 'science' which had not faced up to the problems of Nietzsche's perspectivism.

One can thus argue that the most important feature of Löwith's interpretation of Weber is that he analyses Weber's philosophy of social science as the foundation of his sociology. This strategic reading of Weber is somewhat unusual because, as Friedrich Tenbruck (1980) has constantly complained, Weber's *Wissenschaftslehre* has been neglected by sociologists. While many students are familiar with the essay on ' "Objectivity" in social science and social policy' (Weber 1949) in the collection edited by Edward Shils and Henry Finch, the importance of Weber's methodological essays for understanding Weber's sociology as a whole has been undervalued. The brilliance of Löwith's approach is that he shows, at least implicitly, that both Weber's analysis of the 'bourgeois capitalist world' and his philosophy of the social sciences flow from a single source, namely the human problems of a world in which God is dead.

Weber accepted Nietzsche's argument that knowledge ('truth') is always knowledge from a particular perspective, that is from the standpoint of a system of values. Because God is dead, there is no grounding by which one perspective could have legitimacy over other perspectives. 'Truth' is therefore provisional and it is practical in the sense that it is relevant to specific aims and purposes. In contemporary terminology because there are no 'grand narratives' (Lyotard 1979), we are confronted with many different, local, conflicting 'truths'. Weber's entire sociology, but especially his commentaries on the problem of understanding (*Verstehend*) the meaning of social actions, was an attempt to come to terms with this problem.

An examination of Weber's substantive historical research, his writing on sociological theory and his essays on the philosophy of social science leaves one with the conclusion that Weber was never able to resolve the epistemological problems of sociology. For example, Weber was unable to provide a satisfactory definition of the ideal type of rational action (Sica 1988) – an ideal type which is fundamental to the whole structure of Weber's sociological work. The ambiguities of Weber's sociology reside in the fact that, while he recognised the problem of Nietzsche's perspectivism, he was reluctant to accept its logical implications that all social science propositions about 'social reality' were purely provisional approximations and that they were products of the particular presuppositions of the scientist. Thus,

> A chaos of 'existential judgments' about countless individual events would be the only result of a serious attempt to analyze reality 'without presuppositions' . . . . Order is brought into this chaos only on the condition that in every case only a *part* of concrete reality is interesting and *significant* to us, because only it is related to the *cultural values* with which we approach reality.
>
> (Weber 1949: 78)

In order to try to make this construction of presuppositions scientifically systematic, Weber developed the ideal type as a selection from reality, and tried to establish a coherent

approach to concepts such as ethical neutrality, value judgement and value relevance, but it is very doubtful that this
attempt at clarification was genuinely successful. However,
what emerges from his deliberations is the conviction that
social science cannot be presuppositionless, that value judgement is inevitable, and that the 'laws' of history were merely
heuristic devices. The result was a devastating critique of the
claims made by Marxists that political economy was an exact
science which could predict the collapse of capitalism with
precision. The 'economic interpretation' of history was merely
a one-sided perspective which could be challenged by an
equally one-sided spiritual interpretation.

The significance of Weber's extreme form of nominalism and
constructivism is not what it tells us about his methodological
agnosticism, but what it tells us about Weber's 'ontological
insecurity' (Giddens 1990: 92). As Löwith points out, Weber's
methodological scepticism emerges out of his bleak view of
'man' in bourgeois society:

> The ideal typical 'construct' is based upon a human being
> who is specifically 'free of illusions', thrown back upon itself
> by a world which has become objectively meaningless and
> sober and to this extent emphatically 'realistic'.
>
> (Löwith 1982: 38)

Weber's methodological individualism meant that social science
concepts such as the economy and the state could not be
interpreted as referring to objective, substantive phenomena.
However, Weber's criticisms were not simply suggesting that
collectivist, reified concepts were unscientific. He objected to
the reification of concepts 'because such a view would be enmeshed in transcendent prejudices and ideals, while the world
in which we are situated no longer justifies prejudices of that
particular sort' (Löwith 1982: 39).

Now the meaningless of this world has, according to Weber,
been brought about paradoxically as a consequence of rationalisation. As the world has become more routinised and rationalised, so it has become more disenchanted. Rationalisation has
destroyed the magic garden of faith and certainty, but it has
not produced an alternative set of values which are credible.
Science itself is not a value system, because it is primarily
concerned with means rather than with ends. As the reflexive

rationalism of the process of modernisation has cut away the roots of the old monotheistic faiths, we are left in a world of competing, incommensurable values. Weber thus saw modern societies as cultural arenas within which there was a struggle between polytheistic values for social dominance.

Given deeply seated ontological insecurity, what responses might be possible on the part of a human being? In Weber's sociology, we find many clues and answers which were never presented in a single place. However, the two essays on 'Science as a vocation' and 'Politics as a vocation' (Gerth and Mills 1991) provide us with a reasonably systematic summary. Weber was highly critical of those social groups or movements which sought to escape from the reality of this existential dilemma by for example retreating into the arms of the Church. Weber also rejected the possibility of embracing the Party. Marxism for Weber involved a further rationalisation of life by regulating the market, controlling investment and centralising authority. Marxism would intensify the negative impact of instrumental rationality on the life-world. He was equally critical of the emerging Freudian solution which sought a 'hygienic' answer to ethical dilemmas. He had more sympathy with the eudamonian and erotic response of the followers of Otto Gross who created small effective communities in search of sexual authenticity.[6] Weber was also impressed by the prophetic writings of Stefan George and the circle of influential philosophers and artists that gathered around George at Heidelberg, but Weber could not believe that prophetic poetry was an adequate response to the rationalised world of bourgeois capitalism (Stauth and Turner 1992).

Weber's own response to the crisis of perspectivism can be found in his discussion of 'personality' and in 'the ethic of responsibility', both of which are discussed by Löwith. As we will notice, Weber's response has a close affinity to Heidegger's view that responsibility and calling are necessary features of an adequate orientation to the daunting contingency of our being-in-the-world. Although human beings can never fully escape from the iron cage of the rationalised world of bourgeois capitalism, we have a duty to face up to this reality and in the process we become committed to the development of personality.

Now by 'personality', Weber does not have in mind a

psychological construct. Rather 'personality' refers to a life-plan or a structure within which the chaotic events of the life-cycle can be located. A 'personality' is an organisation of life-events which permits an individual to mature and develop. In this respect, Weber's 'personality' may have much in common with the ideal of the educated and civilised person of the educated middle classes of Germany (*Bildungsbürgertum*) and can also be seen as the sociological legacy of Goethe's *Bildungsroman*. Weber's view is that authenticity consists in 'facing up to reality' and in making a conscious choice about a life-style which can be rationally defended. Authentic personality involves a certain degree of isolation and separation in order to bring up a reflexive ordering of one's own personal and social reality. Weber's model of charismatic authority and authenticity has a close relationship to this heroic image of personality, but it was also captured in his contrast between the 'ethic of ultimate values' and the 'ethic of responsibility'. A rational personality is faced in principle by two competing but viable life-strategies. One can either stand by one's own values, regarding them as having an absolute authority, and make decisions by reference to these transcendental standards, without regard for consequences and implications. Alternatively, it is possible to organise one's life by reference to responsibility for more limited objectives and tasks, paying close attention to consequences and implications. Weber felt that the ethic of absolute ends had been rendered impossible and archane by secular social changes. A modern person could really only choose an ethic of responsibility, knowing that our values are not absolute but provisional, not universal but local.

Weber's difficult and hesitant attempts to formulate a response to the modern fragmentation of values and pluralisation of life-worlds were finally expressed in the idea of *Beruf*, namely a calling or vocation. The term clearly has a religious connotation as a calling to service in the work of God. The idea of a 'vocation' is still associated with the idea of a spiritual vocation. Weber, accepting that secularisation was a necessary feature of rationalisation, rejected the possibility of a religious vocation as a personal solution to the meaninglessness of a rationalised social order, and accepted instead that an ethic of responsibility was perhaps best expressed through either a vocation in politics or a vocation in science. These concepts were fully articulated in two public lectures which Weber gave towards the end of his life in which he challenged the youth of a defeated Germany to face up to the tasks of their time and their generation: either search for truth and personal authenticity in the contemplative life of the world of science, a world we might add which was presuppositionless, or grasp the harsh and difficult post-war social and economic issues of Germany through a life of political action. One aspect of the tragedy of Weber's own life was that he was unable to fulfil his political ambitions in a life of practical politics and that, while he was a formidable scholar, he had relatively little impact in his own life-time on the development of German social science. As Löwith tersely notes: 'it is characteristic of Weber that he did not in any way found a "school" ' (Löwith 1982: 21).

Weber's existential solution to the crisis of late nineteenth-century German culture was in terms of an ethic of responsibility and in terms of the notion of 'character' or personality. This solution as we have seen is full of complexity and uncertainty. For example, if rationality itself has been questioned by the very process of rationalisation, is it possible to sustain the idea of a rational personality with a life-project and a set of norms about responsibility? In addition to the ambiguities of Weber's ideas about personality, it is also important to keep in mind that Weber's own answers were the cultural product of the *Bildungsbürgertum* tradition. This tradition assumed that a cultivated person should attempt to adhere to a number of civilised criteria of personal existence which included inner loneliness, personal cultivation, responsibility and loyalty. These values were the values of the old German educational elite, but these values were under attack from new social forces and conditions which were broadly associated with urban capitalism (Ringer 1969). In particular, Weber was only too conscious that the processes of specialisation with the rationalisation of society made the achievement of personal integrity and wholeness extremely difficult to achieve. This anxiety was the basis of Weber's pessimistic comments in the conclusion of *The Protestant Ethic and the Spirit of Capitalism* about hedonists without a heart and vocational men without a soul. Specialisation negated the whole tradition of the cultivated personality with broad interests and a general education, namely the enlightenment values of the age of Goethe. The tragic vision which characterises Weber's despair was an effect of social changes in Germany which threatened these honorific standards.

To summarise Löwith's account of Weber and Marx in terms of 'this underlying anthropological concern', there was a fundamental convergence in basic values, but in terms of their response to the alienating features of bourgeois society, there was also a basic divergence. From Weber's philosophy of social science, Löwith showed how the underlying problems of a presuppositionless sociology were connected with Weber's attempt to come to terms with Nietzsche, in particular with the diagnosis of value pluralism and debasement as 'the death of God'. Weber's 'substantive sociology' was consequently shaped and organised around a theme of rationalisation. This historical motif involves the complex of ideas that the world has become secular or disenchanted, that scientific ideas (instrumental rationalisation) pervade everyday life, that there has been a specialisation of social activities and authority, and that finally the world has been rendered increasingly meaningless by the erosion of charisma, religion or enchantment. For Weber, the world is predictable, but without an authoritative purpose, that is without grand narratives.

Within this broad scenario, we might distinguish between a specific and a general issue. Weber responded to the specific crisis of post-war Germany in terms of a nationalistic politics which was designed to minimise the magnitude of Germany's defeat. Weber's political sociology with its emphasis on the strong state, charismatic leadership and plebiscitary democracy was directed to the problem of Germany's position in world politics. When Löwith argued that Weber offered a diagnosis but not a therapy, this observation cannot apply to Weber's orientation to the specific crisis of Germany. Weber's answer may not be entirely palatable, but it was not based on acquiescence, quietism and retreatism. It was not merely a diagnosis: Weber's answer was quite specific: Germany must be a strong state. It was in terms of the macro-cultural characteristics of modern society where Weber adhered to a more pessimistic and negative world-view. For Weber, there was ultimately no clear escape from the iron cage of specialisation and rationalisation. Here the only plausible answer was one of stoical resolve.

The differences between Weber and Marx over these political issues were clear. While Marx also saw the bourgeois capitalist world in terms of self-alienation, Marx's teleology, which was the legacy of Hegel's secularised Christian theology, presented the historical role of the proletariat in terms of a resolution of the contradictions of bourgeois society. The proletarian victory would bring to an end the exploitation of human labour, the divisions of the private and the public realm, and the alienation of human beings. Marx's utopian vision of the end of history is, as Löwith argues, a powerful illustration of the chiliastic imagination which down the centuries has challenged ideologies which have celebrated and legitimised the permanency of existing social relations.[7] Whereas Weber's existential solution was individualistic, inward and despairing, Marx's solution was collectivist, external and hopeful. However, we have to keep in mind that Marx's own views on 'man's self-alienation' were eventually transformed into 'vulgar Marxism' in which the economic base mechanically determines the superstructure, and as Löwith points out, 'This is how Weber also regarded Marxism and combated it as a dogmatically economistic historical materialism' (Löwith 1982: 68).

LÖWITH'S LEGACY

Löwith's work will survive as a sensitive and informed study of Heideggerian existentialism, and also as a study which is located in the European sociological tradition of Weber and Marx. In its own way, Löwith's commentary is simultaneously an analysis of the human condition in bourgeois capitalism, namely an analysis of the paradoxical contingency and rationality, autonomy and alienation of modern times. What Löwith's approach does, in fact, is to question the simplistic dichotomies of spirituality/materiality and idealism/materialism. While 'vulgar Marxism' had constructed Marxism as a deterministic science of the mode of production, Löwith's probing of the anthropological concern of Marx's social theory presented a very different perspective on Marx as a philosopher who sought to comprehend the dilemmas of human beings within the ancient debate about essence and existence. In fact, Marx attempted in the 'Theses on Feuerbach' to throw off the old materialism which was deterministic and mechanical by taking on board the voluntaristic view of action in the old idealism. In this respect, both Weber and Marx emerge as critics of simplistic empiricism. Thus, one aspect of the legacy of Löwith is this sensitive appreciation for the complexity of the idea of 'materiality' in relation to any understanding of existence.

In retrospect we may see one of the great changes in Western philosophy in the twentieth century in terms of the critique of Cartesian dualism, which provided the foundation of Western philosophy since Descartes's publications on method. Descartes's famous foundation for modern science (*cogito ergo sum*) presented the idea of reality as a passive object, which the active, rational mind could comprehend directly without metaphysical presuppositions. Cartesianism was thus the origin of the subject/object division and also the dualism of mind and body. Western thought has wrestled with these ideas for decades, but in the twentieth century there has been, from many starting points, a concerted critique of the principal assumptions of mind/body dualism and the subject/object dichotomy. Husserl's Cartesian meditations have thus been critical for the philosophical development of Heidegger, Ricouer, Merleau-Ponty and Derrida. To simplify the issues, twentieth-century philosophy has broadly argued that reality cannot be separated from the knowing subject, because 'reality' is in some sense 'produced' by the paradigms which seek to understand it, and secondly mind and body are not separate; rather, according to writers like Merleau-Ponty, we are 'embodied'. In a more technical parlance, much of modern philosophy from Nietzsche onwards has been concerned to undermine the philosophical credibility and importance of the transcendental subject. The importance of these developments, especially in the work of Husserl, Lukács and Heidegger, has been captured by Goldmann:

> Man is not *opposite* the world which he tries to understand and upon which he acts, but *within* this world which he is a part of, and there is no radical break between the meaning he is trying to find or introduce into his own existence. This meaning, common to both individual and collective life,

common as much to humanity as, ultimately, to the universe, is called *history*.

(Goldmann 1977: 6)

These philosophical arguments have, as it were, restored the human body to agency and cognition, and they have asserted the importance of factual, everyday reality to our practical embodiment. This attempt to understand everyday life is captured in the terminology of *Lebenswelt* (life-world), habitus and the immediate daily life. These ideas which have been crucial to mainstream philosophy have also found their way into the sociological work of Agnes Heller, Pierre Bourdieu and Jürgen Habermas, but they also played a part in the development of symbolic interactionism and ethnomethodology. The idea of everyday life is important in understanding the temporality of embodiment in a specific place; this idea of the intimate relationship between practice, body and place is fundamental, for example, to Bourdieu's attempt to provide a sociological critique of Kant's individualistic and neutral or disinterested notion of taste (Bourdieu 1984).

In fact the body is crucial as both metaphor and concept in the 'materialism' of Marx and Heidegger, and this common theme further helps us to grasp the original nature of Löwith's approach to Weber and Marx. In this respect, it is absurd to suggest that while Marx and Lukács share a set of ideas about existence in common with Heidegger, there is one critical difference, namely that 'the latter conceived human being metaphysically' (Feenberg 1981: 7). Heidegger's whole philosophy was constructed to bring a final end to metaphysics and his view of existence is specifically materialistic.

In the rather special terminology which Heidegger developed in order to articulate his critical views on abstract notions of Being, he constantly employs the idea of hand and place. Thus, as we have seen already, existence for Heidegger is captured by *Da-sein* ('Being-there'). But *Da-sein* also functions in Heidegger's philosophy as a substitute for 'man' or 'subject'. Similarly, the all-important contrast between *Zuhandenheit* and *Vorhandenheit* perfectly indicates the centrality of the hand in Heidegger's philosophy (Turner 1992). *Zuhandenheit* is the equivalent in some respects of Marx's notion of praxis. *Zuhandenheit* or 'manipulability' literally means 'readiness-to-hand', but it signifies something very special about human beings: their great capacity for manipulating and transforming their material world, namely the practical character of human beings. *Vorhandenheit* (literally 'before the hand' or 'presence-at-hand'), by contrast, is that which is there but also that which presents itself to us as objective reality. *Vorhandenheit* is everything which exists objectively outside or other than *Da-sein*. Presence-to-hand refers to the obstinacy and obduracy of the world of things. For Heidegger, the authenticity of existence or Being (*Da-sein*) is an aspect of the dialectic of readiness-to-hand and presence-to-hand in everyday life. Authenticity appears to be present in the very intimacy of the here-and-now world to the human hand. It is for this reason that Heidegger saw the development of technology such as the typewriter as a reification or alienation of the human capacities for immediacy in the direct manipulability of the readiness-to-hand. Thus, the Heideggerian concern for the authenticity of Being in a world of reified objects is parallel to Lukács's development of the concept of reification from Marx's notion of the fetishism of commodities.

Goldmann argues persuasively that this Heideggerian formula of *Zuhandenheit/Vorhandenheit* functions in Heideggerian philosophy as the counter-part to the Marxist idea of the 'identity of the subject and the object':

> By replacing 'totality' with '*Sein*' ('Being'), and 'subject' with *Da-sein* ('Being-there'), Heidegger creates a terminology which undoubtedly has the advantage of expressing, in the very structure of the formula, both the identity and the relative difference of the two concepts. He is then able to criticise . . . any philosophy which still uses the terms 'subject'-'object' as continuing in the wake of traditional ontology in relation to which his own thought would constitute a radical break.
>
> (Goldmann 1977: 13–14)

Heidegger's analysis of Being cannot be properly described, therefore, as metaphysical. But Heidegger attempted to develop an analysis of authenticity/inauthenticity at the level of ontology rather than of sociology. If there is a difference between Heidegger and Lukács, then it is in terms of Lukács's efforts to understand reification/inauthentication in the historical context of the development of the capitalist mode of production. Here again Weber and Marx could be said to converge, as Löwith suggests, in their critical understanding of capitalism in relation to Being via the concepts of rationalisation and alienation. While both Marx and Weber have an ontological theory about the practical nature of human existence, they attempted to understand the problems of existence in bourgeois capitalism through a profound historical analysis of the development of the Western world through slavery, feudalism and capitalism.

NOTES

1 This new preface to Karl Löwith's *Max Weber and Karl Marx* was written in the department of sociology, Flinders University of South Australia, where I was a Visiting Professor in October and November 1992. I would like to thank the department, and especially Professor Claire Williams, for their generous support. Dr Chris Rojek, the Sociology Editor of Routledge was, as usual, enormously supportive in ensuring that this sociological classic could be published in the Routledge Sociology Classics series. Taking a longer view, this new preface allows me to express my great intellectual debt to scholars who have directly shaped my intellectual development, and without whom I would have never engaged with Marx, Weber and Löwith: Tom Bottomore, Alan Dawe, David Lockwood, John Rex, Alfred Sohn-Rethel and Dennis Wrong. The views expressed in this new preface are, of course, my own.

2 Throughout this discussion of philosophical anthropology in Marx and Weber, I shall use the term 'man' rather than its more appropriate alternatives such as 'humanity' or 'human beings'. Neither Marx nor Weber worked in a context where feminist criticism of sexist language was available. It is not entirely appropriate to correct their language. There is, however, an issue as to whether the underlying assumptions of late nineteenth-century philosophical anthropology gave a privileged perspective to men in its analysis of the human condition.

3 There are reasons to be uncertain about referring to Heidegger as an existentialist. In this preface, I shall follow Löwith (1948) in taking existentialism to be a philosophical perspective which treats the position of human beings as precarious creatures who inhabit a reality which is contingent, which argues therefore that existence precedes essence and which consequently regards the world as meaningless. Existentialism in its modern form is secular in denying that the world is shaped by a divine plan. As a result, one can argue that some aspects of Weberian sociology, with its emphasis

on the ethic of responsibility, personality and choice, are compatible with existentialism (Löwith 1982: 47).

4 Heidegger has been fundamental to the development of contemporary postmodernism. It is, for example, interesting to recall that Gianni Vattimo the author of *The End of Modernity* (1988) was a student of Löwith's at Heidelberg in the 1960s. Vattimo's understanding of postmodernism starts with the problem of history in Nietzsche and Heidegger, a problem which was also crucial to Löwith's understanding of Christian eschatology (Löwith 1946).

5 Lucien Goldmann's neglected but important study of Lukács and Heidegger (1977) should be read in conjunction with Löwith's study of Weber and Marx. I have drawn extensively on this study to understand the complex meanings of reality, existence and materialism in Heidegger and Lukács. Goldmann has also been, perhaps indirectly, concerned with the origins of existentialism in his brilliant commentaries on Pascal in his study of the Jansenist movement in France in *The Hidden God* (Goldmann 1964). Although Goldmann attempts to show how the transformation of the French class structure was a condition of the rise of the deterministic ideology of Jansenist soteriology, the hidden God of seventeenth-century France has a similar function to the dead God of Nietzsche's philosophy of the will. Both doctrines address the forlorn status of 'man' in the universe.

6 There is some evidence that Weber's own marriage was never consummated, but he had a sexual relationship with Elsie von Richthoffen. There is also some indication that towards the end of his life Weber was far more sympathetic to the idea of an erotic response to the meaninglessness of an alienated and rationalised world (Mitzman 1971).

7 Mannheim's analysis of the history of utopian thought, which involved, amongst other cases, a study of the Anabaptists and socialist sects has provided the classical reference point for this debate (Mannheim 1991). In twentieth-century Marxism, Ernst Bloch's monumental *The Principle of Hope* is an outstanding attempt to defend the idea that human beings *qua* human beings can only survive on the basis of some utopian commitment to the future as the Yet-To-Be (Bloch 1969).

REFERENCES

Althusser, L. (1966), *For Marx* (London: Allen Lane).

Althusser, L. and Balibar, E. (1968), *Reading Capital* (London: New Left Books).

Baudrillard, J. (1983), *In the Shadow of the Silent Majorities* (New York: Semiotext(e)).

Beck, U. (1992), *Risk Society: Towards a New Modernity* (London: Sage).

Bloch, E. (1969), *Das Princip Hoffnung* (Frankfurt am Main: Suhrkamp).

Bourdieu, P. (1984), *Distinction: A Social Critique of the Judgement of Taste* (London: Routledge & Kegan Paul).

Derrida, J. (1989), *Of Spirit: Heidegger and the Question* (Chicago: University of Chicago Press).

Durkheim, E. (1958), *Socialism and Saint Simon* (London: Routledge & Kegan Paul).

Farias, V. (1987), *Heidegger et le Nazisme* (Paris: Editions Verdier).

Feenberg, A. (1981), *Lukács, Marx and the Sources of Critical Theory* (Totowa, N.J.: Rowman & Littlefield).

Feuerbach, L. (1957), *The Essence of Christianity* (New York: Harper & Row).

Gerth, H. H. and Mills, C. Wright (eds) (1991), *From Max Weber: Essays in Sociology* (London: Routledge).

Giddens, A. (1990), *The Consequences of Modernity* (Cambridge: Polity Press).

Goldmann, L. (1964), *The Hidden God* (London: Routledge & Kegan Paul).

Goldmann, L. (1977), *Lukács and Heidegger: Towards a New Philosophy* (London: Routledge & Kegan Paul).

Gould, M. (1991), 'The Structure of Social Action: at least sixty years ahead of its time', pp. 85–107, in R. Robertson and B. S. Turner (eds), *Talcott Parsons, Theorist of Modernity* (London: Sage).

Heidegger, M. (1962), *Being and Time* (Oxford: Basil Blackwell).

Heidegger, M. (1977), *The Question Concerning Technology and Other Essays* (New York: Harper & Row).

Hennis, W. (1987), *Max Weber's Fragstellung* (Tübingen: J. C. B. Mohr).

Hindess, B. and Hirst, P. Q. (1975), *Pre-Capitalist Modes of Production* (London: Routledge & Kegan Paul).

Jay, M. (1973), *The Dialectical Imagination. A History of the Frankfurt School and the Institute of Social Research 1923–1950* (Boston: Little Brown).

Kuhn, T. S. (1970), *The Structure of Scientific Revolutions* (Chicago: University of Chicago Press).

Lipsett, M. (1960), *Political Man: The Social Bases of Politics* (New York: Doubleday & Company).

Löwith, K. (1928), *Das Individuum in der Rolle des Mitmenschen* (Tübingen: Mohr).

Löwith, K. (1945), 'Nietzsche's doctrine of Eternal Recurrence', *Journal of the History of Ideas*, vol. 6: 273–84.

Löwith, K. (1946), 'The theological background of the philosophy of history', *Social Research*, vol. 13: 51–80.

Löwith, K. (1948), 'Heidegger: problem and background of existentialism', *Social Research*, vol. 15(3): 345–69.

Löwith, K. (1951), 'Skepticism and faith', *Social Research*, vol. 18: 219–36.

Löwith, K. (1952), 'Nature, history and existentialism', *Social Research*, vol. 19: 79–94.

Löwith, K. (1953), *Heidegger: Denker in Dürftiger Zeit* (Frankfurt: Klostermann).

Löwith, K. (1954), 'Man's self-alienation in the early writings of Marx', *Social Research*, vol. 21: 204–30.

Löwith, K. (1959), 'Curriculum vitae', *Archives de Philosophie*, vol. 37: 181–92.

Löwith, K. (1964), *From Hegel to Nietzsche: The Revolution in Nineteenth-Century Thought* (New York: Holt, Rinehart & Winston). *Von Hegel zu Nietzsche. Der Revolutionäre Bruch im Denken des neunzehnten Jahrhunderts* (Hamburg: Felix Meiner Verlag, 1941).

Löwith, K. (1966), *Nature, History and Existentialism and Other Essays* (Evanston, Ill.: Northwestern University Press).

Löwith, K. (1970), *Meaning in History* (Chicago and London: University of Chicago Press).

Löwith, K. (1981), *Samtliche Schriften* (Hamburg: J. B. Metzlersche Verlagsbuchhandlung), 9 volumes.

Löwith, K. (1982), *Max Weber and Karl Marx* (London: George Allen & Unwin). 'Max Weber und Karl Marx', *Archiv für Sozialwissenschaft und Sozialpolitik*, vol. 66, 1932: 53–99 and 175–214.

Löwith, K. (1986), *Mein Leben in Deutschland vor und nach 1933* (Stuttgart: Metzler Verlag).

Löwith, K. (1988), 'My last meeting with Heidegger in Rome, 1936', excerpted from K. Löwith (1986), *Mein Leben in Deutschland vor und nach 1933* (Stuttgart: Metzler Verlag). Reprinted in R. Wolin (1988), 'Martin Heidegger and politics: a dossier', *New German Critique*, no. 45: 91–134.

Lukács, G. (1971), *History and Class Consciousness* (London: The Merlin Press).

Lyotard, J. F. (1979), *La Condition Postmoderne: Rapport sur le Savoir* (Paris: Minuit).

Mannheim, K. (1991), *Ideology and Utopia* (London: Routledge).

Marx, K. (1964), *The Economic and Philosophical Manuscripts* (London: Lawrence & Wishart).

Mitzman, A. (1971), *The Iron Cage: An Historical Interpretation of Max Weber* (New York: The Universal Libarary).

Mommsen, W,. (1989), *The Political and Social Theory of Max Weber* (Cambridge: Polity Press).

Poulantzas, N. (1973), *Political Power and Social Classes* (London: New Left Books).

Ringer, F. K. (1969), *The Decline of the German Mandarins: The German Academic Community 1890–1933* (Cambridge, Mass.: Harvard University Press).

Schumpeter, J. A. (1934), *The Theory of Economic Development* (Cambridge, Mass.: Harvard University Press).

Sica, A. (1988), *Weber, Irrationality and Social Order* (Berkeley: University of California Press).

Simmel, G. (1991), *Schopenhauer and Nietzsche* (Urbana and Chicago: University of Illinois Press).

Stauth, G. and Turner, B. S. (1988), *Nietzsche's Dance: Resentment, Reciprocity and Resistance in Social Life* (Oxford: Basil Blackwell).

Stauth, G. and Turner, B. S. (1992), 'Ludwig Klages (1872–1956) and the origins of critical theory', *Theory, Culture & Society*, vol. 9(3): 45–63.

Tenbruck, F. (1980), 'The problem of the thematic unity in the works of Max Weber', *British Journal of Sociology*, vol. 81(3): 316–51.

Tribe, K. (ed.) (1989), *Reading Weber* (London: Routledge).

Troeltsch, E. (1931), *The Social Teaching of the Christian Churches* (New York: Macmillan).

Turner, B. S. (1981), *For Weber, Essays in the Sociology of Fate* (London: Routledge & Kegan Paul).

Turner, B. S. (1987), 'A note on nostalgia', *Theory, Culture & Society*, vol. 4(1): 147–56.

Turner, B. S. (ed) (1990), *Theories of Modernity and Postmodernity* (London: Sage).

Turner, B. S. (1992), *Regulating Bodies: Essays in Medical Sociology* (London: Routledge).

Turner, S. and Käsler, D. (eds) (1992), *Sociology Responds to Fascism* (London: Routledge).

Vattimo, G. (1988), *The End of Modernity: Nihilism and Hermeneutics in Post-modern Culture* (Cambridge: Polity Press).

Weber, M. (1932), *The Protestant Ethic and the Spirit of Capitalism* (London: Allen & Unwin).

Weber, M. (1949), *The Methodology of the Social Sciences* (New York: Free Press).

Weber, M. (1976), *The Agrarian Sociology of the Ancient Civilizations* (London: New Left Books).

Wolin, R. (1988), 'Martin Heidegger and Politics: a dossier', *New German Critique*, no. 45 (Fall): 91–134.

Note on the translation

The present text is based upon a translation by Hans Fantel, but we have revised it substantially and we have also added notes and bibliographical information where these seemed likely to be helpful to the English reader. Our additions are indicated by the sign [Eds].

In the Bibliography and notes we have referred to English translations of the works cited where these are available; but in the case of Marx and Engels, where several translations exist, we have usually given a reference to the relevant chapter or section of the text, and we have provided our own translation. We have also retranslated some of the passages cited from Max Weber's writings.

TOM BOTTOMORE
WILLIAM OUTHWAITE

Introduction to the translation

Karl Löwith's study of Weber and Marx, first published in 1932,[1] has remained the major attempt to compare, in a systematic and critical way, some of the basic elements of their social thought. The key to this comparison is to be found in Löwith's claim that both thinkers were preoccupied above all with the question of the cultural significance and consequences of modern Western capitalism, and in his attribution of the differences between them to the influence of contrasting philosophical-anthropological conceptions, expressed by Weber in the idea of 'rationalisation' and by Marx in the idea of 'alienation'.

As Löwith notes at the beginning of his essay, his comparison involves a three-way relation, with himself as the third term. His lifelong preoccupation with Heidegger's existential ontology of human existence led him naturally to interpret Marx and Weber as being centrally concerned with the human condition; not in general, as with much existentialist writing, but under capitalism. In so doing, he provided an important corrective to those views which saw Marx as either a political polemicist or a purely 'scientific' analyst of the laws of motion of capitalism, and which took Weber at face value as an empirical scientist eschewing value judgements and speculative philosophy.

To say, as Löwith does elsewhere, that Weber's sociology as a whole represents '*the* counterpoint to Marx's *Capital*'[2] is not to minimise the differences in their respective analyses, nor to deny their very different personal philosophies of life. Weber can be plausibly represented, as he was by Jaspers in a passage which Löwith cites, as an existential philosopher, whereas expressions of personal *Angst* do not appear in Marx's more confident writings. It is inconceivable that Marx would have explained the motivation of his work as Weber once did: 'I want to see how much I can stand.' Yet only dogmatic 'anti-humanists' could deny that the whole of Marx's work is crucially informed by a philosophy of man,[3] and it seems no less clear that Weber's detailed investigations of 'rationalisation' in diverse areas of modern life point beyond themselves to some conception of Western capitalism as a whole – a conception which inevitably straddles the separation of fact from value, of empirical science from philosophical reflection and the identification of fundamental trends in history, which Weber elsewhere upholds with such force.[4] Weber identifies rationalisation as a fundamental and growing tendency within Western civilisation, a tendency which draws ever closer the bars of the iron cage of bondage, though paradoxically it also affords the only hope for individuals to retain a limited degree of autonomy.[5]

Löwith does not merely demonstrate the presence of this theme as it breaks through in the interstices of Weber's work; he argues that it represents the fundamental basis of that work. Hence a direct parallel with Marx: 'What ultimately shaped the scientific work of both [Marx and Weber] arose out of an impulse which entirely transcended science as such' (p. 46 below). This was, Löwith claims, a preoccupation with human emancipation, seen by Weber as a matter of rescuing some ultimate human dignity in the face of rationalisation and the 'parcelling-out of the soul', and by Marx as the cause of the proletariat, representing the possibility of general human emancipation. 'It was this passion in their critical attitude and in the impulse behind their scientific work that assured their objectivity [*Sachlichkeit*]' (ibid.).

This is the basis of Löwith's characterisation of Weber's methodology and his philosophy of social science. What Weber understood and presented as philosophical commonplaces, or as necessary postulates of a scientific orientation to the socio-cultural world, are argued by Löwith to be consequences which Weber derived from the historically specific situation of Western capitalism. Ethical subjectivism, for example, has been dispassionately inferred by later philosophers from an analysis of the language in which moral judgements are expressed. For Weber, by contrast, as Löwith puts it:

The . . . 'objective' *in*validity of our ultimate value standards and the absence of obligatory general 'norms' does not inhere in the general nature of science *as such*; rather, this lack stems from the characteristics of that particular cultural epoch which is fated to have eaten from 'the tree of knowledge', to have recognised that *we* 'must ourselves be able to create' the 'meaning' of history.

The same is true, Löwith argues, of Weber's nominalism, sharply expressed, for example, in his claim that the sociologist must conceive of the state only in terms of the probability that certain kinds of individual action will occur. This claim is historically relative – relative, that is, to a state which is 'in Marx's terms, an "abstract universality" set *above* individuals as single private persons'. Löwith goes on: 'Weber misunderstands himself . . . when he insists . . . on the purely "methodological" significance of his "individualistic" and "rational" definition and denies its substantive character [i.e. its historical specificity] as well as its value-relatedness.'

The value which sustains this definition (and the many others like it in Weber's sociology) is basically that of freedom and autonomy. 'The ideal-typical "construct" is based upon a human being who is specifically "free of illusions", thrown back upon itself by a world which has become objectively meaningless.'

In interpreting Weber's philosophy in this way, Löwith departed fairly radically from Weber's conscious intentions. It is certainly true that Weber saw 'Western' science as a contingent product of a certain historical development, and something which might only be valued by those interested in truth. Nevertheless, he clearly believed that this conception of science 'lies, as we like to think, in a line of development having universal significance and value'. It is perhaps an accident that we ate from the tree, but we cannot unlearn what we have learned, except at the price of self-deception and personal inauthenticity. Those who 'cannot manfully [*sic*] bear this fate of the time' should abandon science and return to the 'old churches'.[6] Weber's tone is kindly, but ultimately contemptuous. At a more technical level, but none the less linked to this general conception of rationalised science, the nominalist principle that 'concepts are primarily means of thought for the intellectual mastery of empirical data' is 'the basic principle of the modern theory of knowledge which goes back to Kant' and can be criticised only on the basis of an 'old-fashioned and scholastic epistemology'.[7] There *is* an existential choice behind the pursuit of modern science, but there is also more than this.

Löwith is perhaps best seen, then, as deliberately going beyond Weber's explicit philosophy of science to develop a more reflective and dialectical conception in which the knowledge of the world furnished by modern science is itself conditioned by the nature of the modern capitalist world. This would bring Weber closer to Marx, at least on a reading of Marx which sees him as committed both to a kind of philosophical realism and to a dialectical conception expressed, for example, in his concept of abstract labour as something which has 'made its way from reality into the textbooks'. It seems, however, that Löwith's treatment of Marx's philosophy of science is less secure and convincing than his handling of Weber. He seems to equivocate between an unclarified conception of 'Marx as a Hegelian' (who would be open to the sort of criticisms Weber levels at Roscher and Knies) and a more Weberian, ideal-typical formulation of Marx's propositions.

If, nevertheless, Löwith's attempt to relate Marx to Weber, at this philosophical level, remains one of the most outstanding and stimulating achievements in the genre, his study seems less successful in bringing to light the differences between them in respect of their sociological and political conceptions. There is indeed a marked asymmetry in Löwith's study, for while his discussion of Marx leads necessarily to the idea of the proletariat as an expression of human self-alienation, and so introduces implicitly the notion of the proletariat as a *political* force which can overcome alienation, there is no corresponding reference to the political forces which Weber regarded as pre-eminent and to which he committed himself. Only at the very end of his monograph does Löwith give a brief, negative characterisation of Weber's political ideas, when he says that Weber 'presented some unpalatable truths to his own class', about its political effectiveness, and on the other hand, questioned the socialist view that the abolition of private enterprise would end the domination of man by man.

Yet the texts from which Löwith quotes here – Weber's inaugural lecture of 1895 and his lecture on socialism of 1918

– make quite clear Weber's positive commitment to the German nation state. In the inaugural lecture he asserted uncompromisingly that the basic principle of his political theory was 'the absolute primacy of the interests of the nation state', which provide 'an ultimate standard of value' in both politics and economics. This view, which undoubtedly guided all Weber's political studies, was reiterated towards the end of his life in the lecture on socialism, which he concluded by saying that 'the question is only whether this socialism will be of such a kind that it is bearable from the standpoint of the interests of the state, and in particular at the present time, of its military interests'.

There are, one might say, *two* Max Webers. The first, by far the most familiar as a result of later exposition and interpretation, is the liberal individualist, preoccupied with the fate of human beings in what he pessimistically foresaw as the iron cage of the future, constituted by machine production, by the inexorable power of material goods – a 'mechanised petrifaction' – and reinforced, as he came to believe, by an equally inexorable extension of bureaucratic regulation. This strand in Weber's thought is also expressed positively in his growing intellectual opposition to the process of 'rationalisation'; an opposition nourished by the aristocratic philosophy of Nietzsche,[8] and to a lesser extent by the neo-romanticism of the Stefan George circle and by his association with utopian socialist communities just before and during the First World War.[9]

The other Weber, who has been revealed more fully by recent studies[10] – though he was already recognised by contemporaries – is the ardent nationalist, obsessed with the need for strong political leadership to establish and maintain Germany's position as a world power; a man who, in Mommsen's words, 'never envisaged any other world than his own, which was largely characterised by the rivalry of nation states'.[11]

These two *personae* seem difficult to reconcile, for the aim of a strong expansionist state engaged in struggles for power implies in practice the subordination of the individual to an authoritarian, and even military, kind of regulation. It is perhaps this very irreconcilability which mainly accounts for the pathos of Weber's life and work as a whole. Yet there is at least one frail bridge between these seemingly antithetical intellectual orientations, provided by the idea of 'charisma'. On one side this notion conforms with Weber's view that it is the value-orientated actions of individuals, or small groups of individuals, which bring about significant changes in society and culture, and his consequent emphasis upon individual responsibility. On the other side, it is the basis for his conception – indebted to Nietzsche's doctrine of the 'superior individual' – of charismatic domination and a 'plebiscitarian leader-democracy', which would produce the dynamic and effective leadership necessary for the promotion of national interests.

By contrast, Marx's thought seems to be more of a piece. His underlying philosophical-anthropological conception of alienation leads directly to the idea of an alienated class, compelled into inhuman conditions of existence, which will necessarily revolt against those conditions and by so doing emancipate not only itself but the whole of society. Marx's analyses in every field, therefore, have a systematic relation to his basic view of the human labour process and its alienation.

This difference between Weber and Marx no doubt accounts in large measure for the very different fates that befell their ideas. Marx's social theory became interwoven with the development of the most important political movement of modern times and has had a profound political influence, though often in forms which would perhaps have surprised and even dismayed him. Weber's thought, on the contrary, seems to have had little political or cultural effect. It may have given some encouragement to imperialist views among the German middle class, but it was hardly the major influence in that sphere. On the other side, it cannot be said to have promoted a politically effective liberal outlook, perhaps because of Weber's own contradictory stance and his underlying pessimism, which made him, as Mommsen says, 'a liberal in despair'. Weber's intellectual legacy became largely confined within the academic discipline of sociology and, partly through the kind of misunderstanding of it that Löwith emphasises, its connections with major political and cultural movements were almost completely severed.[12]

It may well be, however, that some important elements of Weber's philosophical-anthropological outlook, especially his relativistic rejection of any claim to establish a definitive interpretation of history and his profound pessimism about the future development of industrial societies, will acquire – have already begun to acquire – greater prominence and a growing cultural, if not directly political, influence in the closing decades of the twentieth century. There are indications, notably in the writings of Marcuse, and more generally in the work of the later Frankfurt school, of a deep vein of cultural pessimism in modern Marxist thought; and it is no longer quite inconceivable that a Marxist social theorist might say – in stark contrast with Marx himself, still imbued with the nineteenth-century faith in progress, but in harmony with Weber – that he pursues his studies to see 'how much I can stand'. The grounds of this pessimism are, of course, different and in some degree anti-thetical. It is not the prospect of bureaucratic socialism, but the apparent failure of socialism as a project of human emancipation to be accomplished through the agency of the proletariat, which weighs upon the spirit of this *fin-de-siècle* Marxism. And if some ground for hope is sought it is clearly not in Weber's vision of the 'charismatic leader', inextricably bound up with the idea of a powerful nation state, but in the notion of a general 'emancipatory interest' which harks back to Marx's early writings.[13]

NOTES

1 In the *Archiv für Sozialwissenschaft und Sozialpolitik*, vol. LXVI, 1932, pp. 53–99, 175–214. The study was reprinted, slightly revised, in Löwith, 1960, pp. 1–67. In the present translation we have followed the revised text except that we have retained one or two footnotes which were deleted there.

2 'Die Entzauberung der Welt durch Wissenschaft', *Merkur*, June 1964, p. 504.

3 See, for example, Plamenatz, 1975, and Petrović, 1967, pt II.

4 For another view of this situation, see Wilson, 1977, esp. ch. 7.

5 See the discussion on pp. 75–80 below.

6 Weber, 1922, p. 155.

7 Weber, 1904b, p. 106.

8 See especially Eugène Fleischmann, 'De Weber à Nietzsche', *Archives européennes de sociologie*, vol. V, 1964, pp. 190–238.

9 For an account of Weber's 'retreat from ascetic rationalism', see Mitzman, 1970, pt II, ch. 9.

10 See especially Mommsen, 1959 and 1974.

11 Mommsen, 1974, p. 37.

12 Though some politically engaged sociologists were undoubtedly influenced by Weber's ideas; the two outstanding examples, repre-

senting very different political positions, are Raymond Aron and C. Wright Mills.

13 See especially the exposition of this notion in the writings of Jürgen Habermas, more particularly in *Knowledge and Human Interests*.

Chapter 1

Introduction

STATEMENT OF THE PROBLEM

Like our actual society, which it studies, social science is not unified but divided in two: *bourgeois sociology* and *Marxism*. The most important representatives of these two lines of inquiry are Max Weber and Karl Marx. But the sphere of their investigations is one and the same: the 'capitalist' organisation of a modern economy and society. This common problem is becoming increasingly apparent in recent sociological investigations.[1] This field of inquiry became a problem, and indeed a fundamental problem, not only because it comprises a specific problematic of economy and society demanding separate treatment, but primarily because this theme involves contemporary man in the whole of his humanity as the fundamental basis of both social and economic questions.

Only because it is in man as such that the problematic nature of the bourgeois-capitalist social and economic system develops and manifests itself can 'capitalism' itself be grasped in its fundamental significance and made the object of an inquiry within the realm of social philosophy. Since it is necessarily man whose mode of humanity is revealed in the forms of the social and economic conditions of life, a thematically more or less separate analysis of capitalist 'economy and society', i.e. the capitalist 'process of production', will be explicitly or implicitly based on a certain view of the human being who is economically active in this form rather than any other. As a critical analysis of human economy and society, such an inquiry will at the same time be guided by an 'idea' of man, which is distinct from the factual situation. One must ultimately refer back to this idea of man if the 'sociological' investigations of Weber and Marx are to be understood in their fundamental and radical significance. 'To be radical is to grasp things by the root. But for man the root is man himself.'[2] The radically this-worldly view of man expressed here is a presupposition for both Marx and Weber. 'Man, who has found in the fantastic reality of heaven, where he sought a supernatural being, only his own reflection, will no longer be tempted to find only the semblance of himself – a non-human being – where he seeks and must seek his true reality' (Marx).[3] We have therefore the following task: to set out the similarities and differences in Marx's and Weber's idea of man as the basis of economy and society. This is to be accomplished through a comparative analysis of the basic themes of their investigations. Such a comparison cannot lead to agreement, for as long as this-worldly life is 'based on itself and is understood in its own terms', it can only know 'the impossibility of decision in the combat between the ultimate conceivable orientations to life'.[4] The comparison can and should use the shared assumptions to make the differences clear.

Such a comparison has three presuppositions. Comparison as such presupposes first of all that Marx and Weber are 'comparable' in terms of personality and achievement – that they are of comparable stature. Secondly, a comparison of one thing with another assumes that the objects compared are identical in certain respects while differing in others. And thirdly, a comparison of one with another (by us as a third party) presupposes that their respective *goals* of research should be distinguished with regard to their idea of man; this was not the deliberate and explicit goal in the research of Marx and Weber, but it was, nevertheless, their original motive.

The expressly stated subject of the scientific investigations of Marx and Weber is 'capitalism', yet the motive for its study was the question of the fate of man in the contemporary human world, whose problematic nature is characterised by the term 'capitalism'. This question concerning the contemporary human world, implicit in the question of capitalism, in turn implies a definite notion of what it is that makes man 'human' within the capitalistic world – of what constitutes man's humanity in such a world. To represent the motive of Marx's and Weber's research from this perspective does not signify that this motive must have been the guiding intention for them, but assumes it as the permanent background from which they posed their questions. Thus, for example, the obvious intention of the *Communist Manifesto* is practical-political while the intention of Weber's studies in the sociology of religion is theoretical-historical. Yet this does not preclude the possibility that the basic and original motivation for both Weber's historical 'research' and Marx's *Manifesto* may, nevertheless, have been the one single and profound question concerning our contemporary mode of being human. Parallels might then be drawn, for example, between the agitational critique of the 'bourgeois' in Marx's *Manifesto* and the no less 'critical' analysis in the first of Weber's studies in the sociology of religion, in which the same 'bourgeois' human being is quite differently evaluated. Both critiques concern us ourselves in our historical situation.

If this principle of comparison is not arbitrary but central to the substance of their work, then this single question must emerge again and again in the thematically different works of Marx and Weber. It will have to be illustrated, for example, by Marx's first contributions to the *Rheinische Zeitung*[5] no less than by his *Capital*, and by Weber's methodological essays on Roscher and Knies as well as his sociology of religion.

Yet this underlying anthropological[6] concern is not clearly apparent. It remains obscured – in Weber's case by the emphasis on value-free science (*Wissenschaftlichkeit*) and in Marx's case by the emphasis on revolutionary 'praxis'. In choosing this idea as the guiding concept of this comparison between Marx and Weber, we must demonstrate the explanatory power of our principle by selective emphasis on those elements in the work of the two authors which are accessible in these particular terms.

GENERAL CHARACTERISATION OF WEBER AND MARX

To assert the comparability of Weber and Marx – which is our first thesis – in itself requires justification. The enormous difference in the type and magnitude of their impact would seem to preclude the possibility of comparison. *Capital* and the *Communist Manifesto* made Marx a historical force of international importance: Marx has become Marxism. By contrast Weber's theoretical works in sociology, political science, economics and economic history, as well as his topical political writings, have failed to generate further developments even within the narrow confines of their own field – that of social science and the analysis of contemporary politics. It is characteristic of Weber that he did not in any way found a 'school'.[7] A whole class of contemporary humanity derives its notion of its historical human purpose from the writings of Marx, transformed into a world-historical force by Lenin. Yet Weber, only a short time after his death, appears as the outmoded representative of political and economic 'liberalism',[8] as the self-contradictory representative of a waning bourgeois epoch, as the man 'who always returns when an era, near its end, once more takes stock of its worth'.[9]

Yet despite this obvious lack of broad influence, Weber's life and his fragmentary work nevertheless encompass the totality of our time. Like Marx, he assimilated enormous masses of scientific material and he followed the political events of his day with the same passion. Both Marx and Weber had at their command the gift of demagogic style and action, yet both have also written almost unreadable works, whose lines of thought seem often to peter out, being overburdened with supportive material and footnotes. With extravagant and remorseless care, Weber follows up the theories of obscure contemporary mediocrities, while Marx smokes out the hornets' nest of the 'Holy Family'.[10] Both Marx and Weber pile scientific acerbity and personal animus upon seeming trivialities; short articles grow into unfinished books. Thus the question arises: what is the vital impulse behind such vehemence, which is aimed equally at an everyday legal case, an academic appointment, or a book review – or at the future of Germany? Or invested equally in a quarrel with the Rhenish censorship[11] or with Herr Vogt,[12] or brought to bear on Lassalle and Bakunin and the fate of the international proletariat.[13]

The answer is clearly that what was at issue in each case was a 'totality' which was therefore always the same. For Weber this was the rescuing of an ultimate human 'dignity'; for Marx it was the cause of the proletariat. For both it was therefore something akin to human emancipation.

It was this passion in their critical attitude and in the impulse behind their scientific work that assured their objectivity towards the phenomena they investigated.[14] Marx concludes the preface to his doctoral dissertation with a Promethean allusion: 'Against all heavenly and earthly gods.'[15] Self-reliance was also the basis of Weber's critical attitude towards the religious tendencies of the group that had formed around Stefan George[16] – although the atheism of the two men was profoundly dissimilar. What ultimately shaped the scientific work of both arose out of an impulse which entirely transcended science as such. This was not only true of Marx, who was led from the academic career he had planned into politics, but also of Weber, who was led in the opposite direction from politics to science.

A specific topic of Weber's investigations was the inner-worldly meaning of prophecy. Yet Weber, who in his analysis of the old Jewish prophets partly explicated his own work,[17] rejected the *Communist Manifesto* precisely on the ground that it appeared to him a 'prophetic document', and not only 'a scientific achievement of the first rank'.[18] (Paradoxically, it was the aim of the *Manifesto* to differentiate itself from 'utopian' socialism by basing its own prophecies on purely 'scientific' insights.)

The essential motive behind the 'historical' investigations of both Marx and Weber was direct recognition of contemporary 'reality', oriented towards the possibility of political intervention. Both men combined the charisma of the prophet with the skills of 'journalism, advocacy and demagoguery', which Weber regarded as typical of the modern professional politician. Yet for Weber, 'science' and 'politics' remained separate because, although he adopted the position of a 'specialist' in both fields, he transcended science in the narrow sense of specialisation and politics in the narrow sense of partisanship. Marx, by contrast, combined science and politics within the unity of 'scientific socialism', a theoretical praxis and a practical theory.[19] In their reflection on the division and the unity of science and politics, Weber as well as Marx encompassed the totality of theoretical and practical conduct. By this token, both were something other and something more than mere theoreticians; yet both were 'scientists'.

In his youth, Marx said of himself: 'Ideas which our mind has conquered . . . to which reason has welded our conscience, are chains from which we cannot break away without breaking our hearts; they are demons which man can vanquish only by submitting to them.'[20] Weber might have said the same of himself as he followed his own 'demon'. As men of science whose reason was welded to their conscience, both Marx and Weber might be called philosophers in an unusual sense, though neither was a lover of 'wisdom'. Because they were philosophers in a special way – without wanting to be philosophers – they saw academic philosophy as 'logic' and 'epistemology' – in other words, 'professional philosophy'.

> To many of us Max Weber appeared to be a philosopher . . . But if he was a philosopher, he was so as perhaps the only one of our time, and in a different way from what generally constitutes a philosopher today . . . In his personality the whole age, its movement and its problems are present; in him the forces of the age have an exceptionally vigorous life and an extraordinary clarity. He represents what the age is . . . and to a large extent he is the age. In Max Weber we have seen the existential philosopher incarnate. While other men know in essence only their personal fate, the fate of the age acted within his ample soul . . . His presence made us aware that even today spirit can exist in forms of the highest order.[21]

This judgement of Weber by a contemporary is echoed in a contemporary judgement of Marx:

> He is a phenomenon who made a considerable impression on me, although I am active in the same field; in short, prepare yourself to meet the greatest, perhaps the only genuine philosopher now living, who will shortly, when he appears in public (both in his writings and as a lecturer) draw the eyes of Germany upon himself . . . I have always longed for such a man as a teacher in philosophy. Only now do I realise what a dolt I am in the true realm of philosophy.[22]

Neither the sociology of Marx, nor that of Weber, was confined by the boundaries of specialisation. Yet it would be wholly mistaken to construe the fundamental universality of their sociological problematics as a mere 'sociologism' exceeding the limits of sociology as a specialised discipline. In reality, their approach expressed the transformation of Hegel's philosophy of objective spirit into an analysis of human society.

Granted, *Capital* claimed to be nothing but a critique of bourgeois 'political economy', and Weber's sociology nothing but a
specialised science.

> But it is an odd specialised science: it lacks a specific area
> of its own. All its concerns have been treated before by other
> specialised sciences, which are in fact *merely* specific. Thus
> sociology is a specialised science which in fact becomes uni-
> versal. Like the 'grand' philosophy of the past, it subsumes
> all sciences within itself and fertilises all sciences, as long as
> these sciences . . . are in any way concerned with man.

This type of sociology is

> the scientific form which self-knowledge tends to assume in
> the modern world, i.e. as social self-knowledge . . . Max
> Weber admired Marx's materialist interpretation of history,
> which was the first step in the self-knowledge of capitalism,
> as a scientific discovery which decisively influenced his own
> views.[23]

Thus both Marx and Weber were essentially sociologists,
namely, philosophical sociologists; not because they founded
any particular 'social philosophy' but because they in fact,
following the basic principle of their work in the face of the
actual problems of our human existence, questioned the totality
of the contemporary life situation under the rubric of 'capitalism'. Both provide – Marx directly and Weber indirectly – a
critical analysis of modern man within bourgeois society in
terms of the bourgeois-capitalist economy, based on the recognition that the 'economy' has become human 'destiny'.

After considering the universal developmental trend of Western culture, Weber pauses to observe: 'Thus it is also with the
most fateful force in modern life: capitalism.'[24] Similarly, Marx
poses the question in *The German Ideology*: 'How is it that com-
merce, which in itself is nothing more than the exchange of
particular products between various individuals and
countries . . . dominates the entire world – a relation
which . . . like fate in antiquity, hovers over the earth and
with its invisible hand . . . creates and destroys empires and
peoples.'[25]

Marx promptly answers his own question by indicating the
way in which men must 'regain control over the manner of

their mutual relations'. Marx proposes a therapy while Weber has only a 'diagnosis' to offer.[26] This difference is expressed in their interpretations of capitalism. Weber analyses capitalism in terms of a universal and inevitable 'rationalisation', which is an inherently neutral perspective but one which is evaluated ambiguously. Marx, by contrast, bases his interpretation on the unambiguously negative concept of a universal but transformable 'self-alienation'. Rationalisation or self-alienation, which are alternative characterisations of the fundamental meaning of capitalism, also encapsulate the character of modern science. As a specialised enterprise, science is also the instrument and expression of this universal destiny. 'Scientific progress is an element – the most important element . . . in that process of intellectualisation which we have been undergoing for millennia and which today is generally evaluated in such an extraordinarily negative way.'[27]

Marx replies similarly to those critics who accuse political economy of 'barbarically tearing apart things which belong together': 'As if this rupture had made its way, not from reality into the textbooks, but rather from the textbooks into reality, and as if the task were the dialectical accommodation of concepts, not the grasping of real relations!'[28] Yet in keeping with a fragmented reality, it is invariably the dominant spirit of the specialised sciences which is normative for our concepts of truth, objectivity and scientificity. Consequently, the critique of the contemporary world of Marx and Weber can only be brought out if one discounts the apparently specialised character of their own scientific works.

NOTES

1 See especially Mannheim, 1929; Landshut, 1929; Freyer, 1930; E. Lewalter, 'Wissenssoziologie und Marxismus', *Archiv für Sozialwissenschaft und Sozialpolitik*, vol. 64, 1930; and 'Die Moral der Soziologie', *Neue Jahrbücher für Wissenschaft und Jugendbildung*, vol. 5, 1931.
2 Marx, 'A contribution to the critique of Hegel's philosophy of right, introduction' [Eds].
3 ibid. [Eds].
4 Weber, 'Science as a vocation', in Gerth and Mills, 1947, p. 152.
5 Published between 1842 and 1843, when Marx was the editor of the paper [Eds].
6 Löwith is here using the word 'anthropological' in the sense of philosophical anthropology. See below, Chapter 3, pp. 91–5 [Eds].

7 cf. P. Honigsheim, 'Der Max-Weber-Kreis in Heidelberg', *Kölner Viertel-jahreshefte für Soziologie*, vol. V, no. 3, 1926.

8 cf. P. Honigsheim, 'Max Webers geistesgeschichtliche Stellung', *Die Volks-wirte*, vol. 29, pp. 205–12; compare this with Freyer, 1930, p. 156.

9 From the poem used as epigram in Marianne Weber's biography of her husband (*Max Weber: A Biography*).

10 Marx and Engels, *The Holy Family or Critique of Critical Criticism*, 1845.

11 Article in the *Rheinische Zeitung*, May 1842, on the debates in the Rhenish Diet on the freedom of the press [Eds].

12 *Herr Vogt*, 1860 [Eds].

13 cf. Karl Marx, *The First International and After* (Penguin, forthcoming) [Eds].

14 In his lectures on science and politics as vocations, Weber himself repeatedly refers to the intrinsic connection between passion and objectivity (Gerth and Mills, 1947, pp. 135 and 137; 84 and 115). The interpretation of this connection is given by Hegel in the introduction to *The Philosophy of History* [Eds].

15 *Differenz der demokritischen und epikureischen Naturphilosophie*, 1841.

16 Stefan George, 1868–1933. German lyrical poet, who had a considerable influence on German cultural life through the *Blätter für die Kunst*, a journal which he founded in 1892, and the 'George-Kreis', a circle of his admirers [Eds].

17 cf. Christoph Steding's dissertation submitted in 1931 at the University of Marburg, 'Politik und Wissenschaft bei Max Weber', which convincingly demonstrates Weber's historical self-interpretation in terms of his view of ancient Jewish prophecy (cf. Weber's *Ancient Judaism*).

18 cf. Weber, 1924b, pp. 255 ff.

19 cf. Luppol, 1929, pp. 8 ff.

20 Marx, 'Der Kommunismus und die Augsburger Allgemeine Zeitung', in the *Rheinische Zeitung*, October 1842.

21 From Karl Jaspers's Commemorative Address on Max Weber; Karl Jaspers, *Max Weber*, 1921, 1926, p. 3. Reprinted in Jaspers, *Rechenschaft und Ausblick*, p. 9.

22 From a letter of Moses Hess to A. Auerbach, 1841. In Hess, 1959.

23 Jaspers, op. cit., pp. 6 ff.; *Rechenschaft und Ausblick*, pp. 11 ff.

24 *The Protestant Ethic and the Spirit of Capitalism*, p. 17.

25 Marx, *The German Ideology*, pt I, section A, 1. Just like Marx, Lassalle also refers to the law of the market as the 'cold, ancient fate of the bourgeois world'.

26 cf. E. Wolf, 'Max Webers ethischer Kritizismus und das Problem der Metaphysik', *Logos*, vol. XIX, no. 3, 1930.

27 'Science as a vocation', in Gerth and Mills, 1947, pp. 138 ff.

28 *Grundrisse*, introduction, section 2.

Chapter 2

Weber's interpretation of the bourgeois-capitalist world in terms of 'rationalisation'

THE STARTING POINT OF WEBER'S RESEARCH

Truth in the turmoil of the bewitched
Who learn it only to exchange it
For new beliefs or to dismember it . . .
Truth without respite on worn-out pillows
Without chewing again the finished fragments . . .
Truth which lays bare even dignity,
Struggling to carry on your shoulders every burden
Of the displaced idols and the contents
Of the hollowed-out firmament and of hell,
This truth you bore out of the ground through a thousand
    doors,
A leader free from the falsehoods to which others are
    drawn.[1]

The field, specifically 'worthy of being known', in which Weber's investigations move, is basically a single one. It is not this or that particular fact, nor the 'general cultural significance' of capitalism. This field, whose scholarly investigation was Weber's aim in the midst of all his methodological consider-ations and his wide-ranging substantive investigations, was the following: 'The social science we wish to pursue is a science of reality (*Wirklichkeitswissenschaft*). We wish to comprehend in its specific quality the reality of the life which surrounds us and into which we are placed – the interrelation and cultural meaning of its individual phenomena in their contemporary form as well as the causes of their having developed in the way they have.'[2] In consequence, it is not the purpose of historical investigation to find out how it was (as in Ranke),[3] nor how it had to be because of historical necessity (as in Marx). Rather, historical investigation should render comprehensible how we are today as we have become. 'Capitalism' is one of the factors, indeed a pre-eminent factor, in this history of the present, which is however itself merely a 'segment of the process of human destiny'.[4]

This apprehension of the 'meaning' of the reality that surrounds and determines us – this socio-historical self-knowledge – is explicitly distinguished by Weber from the search for ultimate 'factors' and general 'laws'.

> The meaning of the form of a cultural phenomenon, and the basis of this meaning, cannot be rendered intelligible in terms of a system of laws, no matter how complete; for meaning presupposes the relations of cultural phenomena to ideas of value. Empirical reality is 'culture' for us, because (and in as much as) we relate it to values; it comprises those elements of reality which are rendered meaningful for us by this relation, and only these elements.[5]

Our human reality can therefore never be comprehended 'without presuppositions'. 'The only thing which would result from the attempt at a seriously "presupposition-less" knowledge of reality would be a chaos of "existential judgements" about innumerable discrete perceptions. And even this result would be only seemingly possible.'[6]

The categorisation of a process as, for example, a socio-economic phenomenon, does not signify anything 'objectively' inherent in the process itself. It is conditioned by the direction of our cognitive interest, which in turn arises from the specific cultural meaning of such a 'process'.[7] This meaning is what it is by being so for us as human beings, though not necessarily for us as singular individuals. But what is meaningful for us 'cannot of course be discovered by a "presupposition-less" investigation of the empirically given; rather, the recognition of its meaningfulness is a prerequisite for anything to become the object of investigation'[8] – a prerequisite even for its appearing problematical and worth knowing. A case in point is the 'fact' of the meaning of 'capitalism'.

Human reality is meaningful for us and 'worth knowing' in various possible respects. This includes the meaningful fact of science itself in its character of having become so-and-not-

otherwise. Weber regards the scientific form of his own cognitive style as a characteristic of the specific historical character
of the whole of our modern existence and of its problems.
This sets him radically apart from any purely scientistic and
unreflective eagerness for specialised knowledge, as well as
from the naive faith in science exhibited by most Marxists.[9]
Weber's awareness of the character of science prompts him to
question the 'meaning' of specialised and rationalised science.[10]
Having become specialised and professionalised, and to that
extent 'positive', science itself has become part of the 'spirit'
and un-spirit of 'capitalism'.[11] Within the framework of such a
science one cannot determine – scientifically – whether such
science has any meaning at all or what sort of meaning it has,
in as much as it is neither a path to 'God', nor to 'True Being',
nor even to personal 'happiness'.

Weber's 'methodological' question as to the value of science
is basically the same question that Nietzsche posed in regard
to *philosophy* when he inquired after the meaning and value of
'truth' – for 'what sense could *our* existence have, if not the
sense that within us this urge toward truth has become conscious of itself *as a problem*?'[12] 'Faith in the value of scientific
truth' is 'the product of particular cultures', observes Weber.[13]
And from this point of departure he posits the requirement of
the so-called value-*freedom* of scientific judgement. This does
not constitute a retreat to pure scientificity; rather it is the
desire to take into account the *extra*-scientific standards within
scientific judgement. What this doctrine demands is not the
elimination of guiding 'value ideas' and interests, but their
objectivation, so as to provide a basis for us to distance ourselves from them. It is a 'hair-thin' line that separates science
from faith[14] and scientific judgement cannot really be categori-
cally *severed* from value judgement, though the two must be
distinguished.

What can and must happen in the interest of scientific 'objectivity' is not an illusory denial of 'subjectivity' but the deliberate
and explicit acknowledgement and consideration of what is
scientifically relevant, although it is scientifically unprovable.
So-called 'objectivity' – and Weber never speaks of objectivity
except as 'so-called' and in quotation marks – 'rests exclusively
on the fact that the given reality is ordered in categories, which
are *subjective* in the specific sense that they constitute the *precon-*

dition of our knowledge and are contingent upon the presupposition of the value of that particular truth which only empirical knowledge can give us'.[15] Consequently, Weber's objection to Marxism as 'scientific socialism' is not that it rests upon scientifically unprovable ideas and ideals, but that the subjectivity of its fundamental premises is presented with the appearance of 'objective', universal validity. His objection is therefore that Marxism *confuses* subjective and objective premisses and thus is scientifically prejudiced in its own value judgements and prejudices. 'The preceding arguments are directed against this confusion, not against the assertion of personal ideals. The absence of principles and scientific "objectivity" have no inner relation to each other.'[16]

According to Weber, Marxism is not too little committed to a belief in science, but far too much. What it lacks is a certain 'scientific open-mindedness' in the face of the questionable nature of scientific objectivity. Weber holds that binding norms and ideals are not scientifically provable and that, in consequence, there are no 'recipes' for praxis; yet it does not follow from this principle 'that value judgements, because they are ultimately "subjective" in origin, lie altogether outside the range of scientific discussion . . . Criticism does not stop in the face of value judgements. Rather, the question is: what is the meaning and purpose of scientific criticism of ideals and value judgements?'[17]

Weber's main purpose, therefore, is as follows: to render the 'ideas', 'for which people in part allegedly and in part actually do struggle',[18] intelligible *qua* 'ideas' by means of scientific critique (e.g. the critique of Roscher and Knies) and through self-reflection. This uncovering of the essentially guiding ideas and ideals of scientific investigations, the unveiling of what is 'ultimately intended', is designated by Weber himself as social philosophy.[19] The ultimate achievement of scientific reflection in this regard is

> to make conscious the ultimate yardsticks manifest in the concrete value judgement,[20] thereby rendering these standards accessible to a process of discussion and argument which is clear about its own premises. Scientific self-reflection, which transcends the naive positivity of specialised science, does not indicate what 'should' be done; but

it does show what can consistently be done with available means to attain a pre-given purpose. Above all, such self-reflection enables us to know what we really want. The here presupposed 'objective' invalidity of our ultimate value standards and the absence of obligatory general 'norms' does not inhere in the general nature of science as such; rather, this lack stems from the characteristics of that particular cultural epoch which is fated to have eaten from 'the tree of knowledge', to have recognised that we 'must ourselves be able to create' the 'meaning' of history. 'Only an optimistic syncretism . . . can deceive itself theoretically as to the tremendous seriousness of this circumstance or evade its consequences in practice.'[21]

If large religious communities and 'prophets' were still in existence, generally accepted 'values' could also exist. But in the absence of these, there is nothing but a struggle between many but equally accredited 'gods', 'ideals', 'values' and *Weltanschauungen*.[22]

In recognition of this same state of affairs, the 'anarchy in all deep convictions', and dispensing with 'metaphysical classroom philosophy', Dilthey attempted to develop generally valid principles out of the 'historical consciousness' itself. Weber, by contrast, not only 'renounced' the derivation of such principles, but actually 'sighed with relief whenever the impossibility of formulating objectively valid value judgements had once again been proved'[23] – his relief corresponding to his idea of 'human freedom'. Precisely because scientific investigation rests upon inexplicit but all-pervading and decisive presuppositions – of a human kind – because the human being is the precondition of the scientist, Weber's task is no longer one of specialised *sociology* but of social philosophy. His aim is to make explicit the *a priori* of the guiding value ideas within each specific inquiry.

Such an investigation must necessarily seem sterile to the specialised scientist, because, as Weber himself occasionally emphasises,[24] it 'yields nothing' – nothing, that is, in terms of positive scientific progress; yet it does lead to a philosophical re-examination of the possible 'meaning' of scientific objectivity and knowledge. The original motive of this reflection is not a concern with a free-running 'methodology'. Rather, this re-examination of the meaning of scientific objectivity arises itself from a specific belief: namely, the disbelief in the traditional value ideas of scientific research. The most general characteristic of these traditional value ideas is their claim to unconditioned objectivity. It is therefore the belief of science in objective norms and their scientific demonstrability which Weber fundamentally attacks with the means of science itself and for the sake of scientific 'open-mindedness'. This open-mindedness is 'scientific' in precisely the sense in which Marx speaks of a 'scientific' approach as a 'critical' one and speaks of both as truly 'human'. Scientific open-mindedness, especially *vis-à-vis* one's own prejudices, characterises for Weber the ethos of theory. Weber sees true human dignity in precisely that approach which draws positive consequences from what is not 'given'. Consequently, his detailed disclosure of 'the ultimately intended', that is, the guiding value assumptions of scientific research, serves a dual purpose: not merely to establish the presence and significance of these assumptions and then to leave them alone, but the much more definite aim of the 'demystification' of their content.

The essential positive purpose of Weber's essays in the philosophy of science is the radical demolition of 'illusions'. The two exemplary treatises on Roscher and Knies involve the methical destruction of certain specific prejudices and value judgements, namely, those which impair 'scientific open-mindedness' by contradicting the fact of human history that 'today's' perspective is essentially secular – that science, as Nietzsche said, is 'scientific atheism'.[25] Weber's 'methodological' treatises spring ultimately from his awareness of this particular situation, that 'after a thousand years of an allegedly or supposedly exclusive orientation toward the magnificent pathos of the Christian ethic, our eyes have become blinded to it'.[26] His essays emerge with an inner logic from his recognition of the questionable character not merely of modern science and culture but of our present orientation to life in general. Weber was quite aware of this underlying motive of his methodological reflections, just as Marx was aware of the fundamental meaning of his specific critique of Hegel's *Philosophy of Right* and its 'method'.

Weber concludes his programmatic treatise on 'the objectivity of knowledge in social and political science' with a defence against the possible misunderstanding that these methodological and conceptual reflections had any significance *per se*. But he is no less negative towards 'fact-grubbers' who are insensitive to the 'refinement of a new thought'. Finally, he provides the following positive justification of the *necessity* of these apparently sterile deliberations:

> In a time of specialisation, all work in the field of cultural science will regard the treatment of its material as an end in itself, once the material has been defined by a specific problematic and some methodological principles have been set up. One then no longer constantly and deliberately measures the cognitive value of discrete facts and findings against ultimate value assumptions: indeed, one altogether ceases to be conscious that these facts are anchored in value assumptions. And it is a good thing that this is so. But at a certain point a different perspective enters: the meaningfulness of unreflectively applied perspectives becomes uncertain, and the way is lost in the dusk. The light of the great cultural problems moves on. Then science too prepares to change its standpoint and its conceptual apparatus and to look down from the heights of thought towards the stream of events.[27]

Thus whenever traditional attitudes and perspectives become uncertain, the methods and conceptual apparatus of science also change. Purely methodological reflections without the formulation and solution of substantive problems seem unfruitful to Weber, but in certain historical situations such reflections become unavoidable and important. This is the case when 'in consequence of strong shifts in the "perspectives", which govern the presentation of a given subject, the notion occurs that the new "perspectives" also entail a revision of the logical forms employed within the traditional "enterprise". This, in turn, produces uncertainty as to the "essential nature" of one's own work. Such a situation unquestionably exists at present in the case of history.'[28]

In his essays on Roscher and Knies, Weber produces a detailed analysis and demystification of ultimate standards of scientific judgement which had become meaningless. He traces back the curious contradictions which he demonstrates in Roscher's works to an unclarified relationship between 'concept and reality'. Ultimately this implies an unclarified relationship between man in the process of attaining knowledge and the reality of our contemporary world. Roscher's analysis of historical events retains everywhere an unexplained 'background'. Roscher does not even intend to explain this 'background', even though it is precisely this residual element which according to him holds everything together. Roscher calls this pervasive background alternately in modern biological terms 'the vital force', and at other times 'the thoughts of God' or suprahuman decisions. The 'emanatistic' character of Roscher's philosophical argumentation[29] is thus ultimately rooted in an unspecified but definite faith in providence, even though Roscher's formulation carefully avoids direct reference to divine order. He does not deduce reality from 'ideas' in the manner of Hegel, but nor does he reduce the knowledge of reality to that which is humanly and 'empirically' provable. Even in economic life he assumes a 'higher' divine element which limits worldly self-interest, and this presupposition also decisively penetrates right into the logical structure of his 'Political Economy', from whence Weber extracts it. Thus Roscher's method remains an inconsistent and self-contradictory structure[30] which corresponds to his 'mild, conciliatory' personality. In no way is his method the expression of 'clear and consistently implemented' ideals. The self-contradiction in Roscher's method arises inherently from the unification of 'scientifically open-minded' inquiry with a 'religious perspective'.

> In relation to Hegel, Roscher represents less a contrast than a retrogression. Hegelian metaphysics and the dominance of speculation have disappeared in him; Hegel's brilliant metaphysical constructions are replaced by a fairly primitive form of simple religious faith. Yet we note here that this goes along with a process of recovery – one might even call it a progress towards open-mindedness in scientific work, or – to employ the awkward current usage – 'freedom from prior assumptions'.[31]

Here it becomes quite evident that Weber's insistence on 'scientific open-mindedness'[32] does not refer merely to 'logical' contradictions or obscurities (as Weber's own words often seem to indicate). Rather, scientific and philosophical practice gains the 'value' of clarity and open-mindedness from the fact that it is an expression of a purely secular attitude towards life oriented towards 'mundane' events. Such an orientation is contrary to Roscher's religious interpretation of history. It is the open-mindedness of not being closed in by transcendent ideals, which characterises Weber's 'empirical' method.[33]

As with Roscher, Weber also makes clear in regard to Knies,

> the fundamental philosophical basis of his concept of 'free-dom' and its consequences for its importance in the logic and method of economics. It is soon evident that . . . Knies also is enmeshed by that historically oriented doctrine of 'organic' natural rights, which in Germany penetrated all areas of research into human culture, primarily under the influence of the historical school of law.[34]

Weber then begins with the following question: what concept of personality is implied by Knies's concept of freedom? Again the answer is highly abstract, yet decisive for the realm of the concrete. Knies presupposes a concept of personality as an individual 'substance'. The formal unity of the personality is surreptitiously transformed by him into organic-naturalistic unity, which he then interprets as being objectively present and free of contradiction. Conjoined with this is a preconception of the nature of 'morality', although – as Weber observes – entire cultural movements such as puritanism have produced a human type characterised precisely by its 'contradictory' ethics. Like Roscher, Knies also encounters everywhere a 'dark back-ground', a kind of unified vital force as the ultimate agent within the historical process and as the principle of historical interpretation. Knies presupposes a substantial and metaphys-ical conception of individuals and peoples 'in accordance with the spirit of romanticism'; Weber calls this 'a paler version of Roscher's pious faith that the "souls" of individuals as well as of peoples are created directly by the hand of God'.[35] Knies also is still under the influence of the epigones of the Hegelian metaphysic of history, which was diverted into the realm of anthropology and biology. This traditional perspective is clear in the 'emanatistic' character of his basic concepts.

The real collectivity and the abstract concept of species over-lap in his work. Nor does he succeed in presenting the relation-ship between concept and reality with scientific open-mindedness.[36] Yet this particular 'failure' does not result from a purely 'scientific' error, such as a lack of logical sharpness.

Rather, this emanatistic 'logic' is in itself the consequence of general metaphysical or ontological premises. These, in turn, are based on what Dilthey has called the vestiges of a metaphysical attitude of humanity to reality.[37]

What Weber actually reveals is not a purely scientific ambiguity. Rather, he points to the fact that Knies is scientifically ambiguous precisely to the extent that he has not yet become fully secular in his orientation. What changes as a result of Weber's rejection of the emanatistic conceptualisations of Roscher and Knies is therefore not merely a logical 'conceptual apparatus'. The change affects the fundamental methodology and, at the same time, the crucial concept of 'reality' itself, which is presented in this particular way by means of this methodology and in these concepts. Along with the transformation of reality into something entirely secular and without an 'objective' meaning, the emanatistic conceptualisation also becomes an ideal-typical 'construction', and all 'substantial' definitions of social 'structures' vanish. The constructivist and 'nominalistic' character of Weber's basic methodological concepts and the whole style of his scientific approach do not arise from an immediate demand of science as such. Nor can this approach be countered in terms of the 'phenomena' (for that would presuppose that phenomena could be addressed only through one *logos*). It is, rather, another consistent expression of a quite specific attitude of humanity towards reality. The ideal-typical 'construct' is based upon a human being who is specifically 'free of illusions', thrown back upon itself by a world which has become objectively meaningless and sober and to this extent emphatically 'realistic'.

This human being is thus forced to attempt its own construction of substantive meaning and meaning-context. It must first of all define its relation to reality as 'its own' – and 'create' meaning in both theoretical and practical terms. Nation, state and individual can then no longer be conceived and interpreted as unified substances with deeper backgrounds – not just because this would be simply unscientific, but because such a view would be enmeshed in transcendent prejudices and ideals, while the world in which we are situated no longer justifies prejudices of that particular sort.

Only in these terms can one understand such positions as Weber's exemplary definition of the existence of the state in terms of the probability that 'certain kinds of social action (namely, the action of individuals) will occur'. It is *de facto* based on the model of a quite specific state-like 'reality' – namely, the modern state within which we are situated.[38] This is a conception of the state as a kind of rational 'institution', an 'enterprise'. In Hegelian terms, it is the *Verstandesstaat*, the 'rational state' of civil society;[39] or, in Marx's terms, an 'abstract universality' set above individuals as single private persons.[40]

Weber misunderstands himself as a specialised scientist when he insists (*vis-à-vis* Spann)[41] on the purely 'methodological' significance of his 'individualistic' and 'rational' definition and denies its substantive character as well as its value-relatedness.[42] What Weber proved in regard to Roscher and Knies holds equally true for himself: ultimate presuppositions and *Weltanschauungen* extend right into the 'logical' structure. Yet the ultimate assumption inherent in Weber's 'individualistic' definition of so-called social 'structures' is this: that today only the 'individual', the self-sufficient single person, is true and real and entitled to existence, because 'objectivities' of all kinds have been demystified (through rationalisation) and no longer have any independent meaning. If the state were indeed still a *res publica* and man as such a citizen of city and state rather than primarily a private person responsible only to himself, then it would be meaningful to interpret the state itself in substantial and 'universalistic' terms and not merely in terms of the chances of its 'existence'. Here again Weber's scientific open-mindedness (*Unbefangenheit*) shows itself as a matter of no longer being enmeshed in transcendent prejudices.

Another of these prejudices, transcendent in the broadest sense and extending far beyond the sober everyday life of a 'disenchanted' world, is also shared by Marxism. It is the faith in objective 'development' and 'progress'.[43] Yet this faith becomes necessary only 'when the need arises to provide a secular but nevertheless objective "meaning" for human destiny once it has been voided of religious content'.[44] According to Weber, this need is inconsistent with secularity. For sober 'reality' now stands in a secular light, and the principle for the interpretation of this sobered world is the process of rationalisation through which the world has disenchanted and sobered itself.

Yet the yardstick by which Weber judges the historical fact

of rationalisation is its apparent opposite, namely, the freedom of the independent self-sufficient individual, the 'human hero', in relation to the excessive weight of the kinds of 'orders', 'institutions', 'organisations' and 'establishments' effected by rationalisation in modern life.[45] This thesis must now be developed more closely by means of an analysis of the original and comprehensive meaning of rationalisation, which is also the counter-concept to Marx's interpretation of the same phenomenon in terms of 'self-alienation'.

RATIONALITY AS THE PROBLEMATIC EXPRESSION OF THE MODERN WORLD

> It is the destiny of our era, with its characteristic rationalis-ation and intellectualisation and, above all, the disenchant-ment of the world, that precisely the ultimate and most sublime values have withdrawn from the public sphere . . .[46]

It has been established that the fundamental and entire theme of Weber's investigations is the character of the reality sur-rounding us and into which we have been placed. The basic *motif* of his 'scientific' inquiry turns out to be the trend towards secularity. Weber summed up the particular problematic of this reality of ours in the concept of 'rationality'. He attempted to make intelligible this general process of the rationalisation of our whole existence precisely because the rationality which emerges from this process is something specifically irrational and incomprehensible.

For example, earning money in order to secure one's stan-dard of living is rational and intelligible. Yet rationalised money-making for the sake of making money, 'conceived purely as an end in itself', is specifically irrational. The elemen-tary and decisive fact is this: every instance of radical rationalis-ation is inevitably fated to engender irrationality. Weber specifically noted this in his reply to a criticism offered by Brentano.[47] There he declared that it is in fact a matter of 'rationalisation in the direction of an irrational way of life'. Only because of this – and by no means 'for its own sake' – is rationalisation a phenomenon which is specifically problem-atic and worth knowing about, rather than merely one phenomenon among many.

Weber demonstrated the fact of rationalisation in its universal and fundamental, world-historical and anthropological significance in his preface to the *Sociology of Religion*, Volume I. The phenomenon of rationalisation is 'the great principle not only for his sociology of religion and methodological essays but of his entire system'[48] – not least his political writings. For him it represents the basic characteristic of the Western way of life in general and – in short – our 'destiny'. One may nevertheless relate to this destiny as variously as Weber and Marx, and hence interpret it differently: from the viewpoint of the sociology of religion or in the perspective of political economy. Even the approach from the standpoint of the sociology of religion aims in the end to be nothing less than a contribution to the sociology of rationalism itself.[49] In explicit contrast and in supposed opposition to Marx's 'economic' analysis, the distinctive character of Weber's analysis of capitalism in terms of the sociology of religion consists of the following: Weber did not regard capitalism as a power made up of 'relations' of the forces and means of production which had become autonomous, so that everything else could be understood therefrom in terms of ideology. According to Weber, capitalism could only become the 'most fateful' power in human life because it had itself already developed within the framework of a 'rational way of life'. The 'rationality' which is claimed as a principle of understanding is thus not only the rationality of something – the rationality of a certain domain (which then also acts as a 'determinant' for other areas of life).

Despite his specialised scientific procedure (in the form of the reversible causal imputation of particular 'factors'), Weber conceived of this rationality as an *original totality* – as the totality of an 'attitude to life' and 'way of life' – which is subject to a variety of causal conditions but is nevertheless unique: as the occidental 'ethos'. This determinant ethos[50] manifests itself in the 'spirit' of (bourgeois) capitalism as well as in that of (bourgeois) Protestantism.[51] Both religion and the economy are formed in their living religious and economic reality within the current of this determinant totality, and they, in turn, concretise this totality by leaving their imprint upon it. The form taken by the economy is not a direct consequence of a particular faith, nor is this faith an 'emanatistic' consequence of a 'substantive' economy. Rather, both are shaped 'rationally' on the basis of a general rationality in the conduct of life. In its primarily economic significance, capitalism *per se* cannot be regarded as the independent origin of rationality. Rather, a rational way of life – originally motivated by religion – let capitalism in the economic sense grow into a dominant force of life. Thus where the tendency toward 'certain kinds of practical-rational life-styles' was absent, 'even the development towards an economically rational way of life met serious internal resistance'.

In the past[52] the formative elements of a way of life included religious forces, and the 'ethical ideas of duty' anchored in a belief in these forces, 'to a degree hardly intelligible today'. Hence Weber searches for the inner connection between the Protestant 'ethic' and the 'spirit' of capitalism. The inner 'elective affinity' (*Wahlverwandtschaft*) between the two is that of an ideology of religious faith and economic action. Both are based on a general 'spirit' or ethos, whose socially distinctive carrier is the Western bourgeoisie.

This general spirit of 'rationality' dominates the arts[53] and sciences as well as the legal, administrative, social and economic life of modern humanity. This universal rationalisation of life entails a system of multiple dependencies, an 'iron cage' of 'subordination', a general subjection of man to an 'apparatus'. Every individual is inescapably integrated into one or another 'enterprise', whether in the economy or in science. And yet (Weber's essay 'Politics as a vocation' closes with such a 'yet'), it is precisely this rationality which for Weber is the locus of freedom. This link between rationality and freedom, which is here only asserted, can be perceived, more directly than in his theoretical investigation, in the inner impulse behind Weber's practical attitude towards all rationalised institutions, organisations and forms of order in modern life: he fights against their claim to metaphysical reality and uses them as means to an end.

In his essay 'Knies and the problem of irrationality' Weber discusses the question of so-called free will in relation to historical investigation:

Time and again one encounters statements that the 'unpredictability' of personal action, considered as a consequence of 'freedom', represents a specific dignity of human beings and hence of history. This view is expressed, either directly or covertly, by presenting the 'creative' significance of the acting personality as a contrast to the 'mechanical' causality of natural events.[54]

In a footnote, Weber comments ironically on Treitschke's and Meinecke's 'reverence' in the face of a so-called irrational 'remnant', an inner 'sanctum' and 'mystery' of the free personality.[55] What Weber wants to demonstrate in his subsequent remarks[56] is by no means the individual's lack of freedom, but rather the 'trivial', 'self-evident' fact, continually forgotten or obscured, that this 'creative' freedom, primarily attributed to man, is not an objectively demonstrable attribute of man. It is something which can be seen only on the basis of a 'value judgement', a specific evaluation, based on a subjective attitude to a set of facts which 'in themselves' are insignificant. In themselves, unpredictability and therefore irrationality are not primary attributes of free human action, contrasted with the predictability of events in nature; in fact, for example, the weather may be less predictable than human behaviour.

> Every military command, every penal statute, indeed every statement we make in our interaction with others, 'counts on' producing certain effects in the 'psyche' of those to whom it is addressed. It does not anticipate an absolute absence of ambiguity in every respect and for all purposes; merely a response adequate to the purpose which the command, the statute, or the concrete utterance in general was intended to serve.[57]

In reality, human conduct becomes less predictable, the less it is free action, i.e. the less control a person has of himself or herself and therefore the freedom of his or her own actions.

> The 'freer' the actor's 'decision' – the more it results from his or her 'own considerations', undistorted by outer compulsion or irresistible 'affects' – the more motivation itself, *ceteris paribus*, falls remorselessly within the categories of 'means' and 'end'. Hence the rational analysis of motivation . . . can succeed more completely. Moreover, the 'freer' the 'action' is in the sense described here, i.e. the less it has the character of a 'natural event', the more the concept of 'personality' comes into play. This concept of personality finds its 'essence' in the constancy of its inner relation to

certain ultimate 'values' and 'life-meanings'. In the course of action, these turn into purposes and are thus translated into teleologically rational action. The increase of such freedom therefore leaves less and less room for that romantic-naturalistic formulation of the concept of personality, which instead seeks the true sanctum of the personality in the dark, undifferentiated, vegetative 'underground' of personal life, i.e. in that 'irrationality' which 'people' have in common with animals. It is this kind of romanticism which lies behind the 'mystery of the personality' in the sense in which it is invoked occasionally by Treitschke and very often by many others and which then, where possible, consigns the 'freedom of the will' to these naturalistic regions. The absurdity of the latter approach is evident even in immediate experience: we 'feel' ourselves to be 'compelled' precisely by those 'irrational' elements of our action . . . or at least partially conditioned by them in a way which is not 'immanent' in our 'will'.[58]

This point becomes even more explicit in Weber's argument with E. Meyer:

It is obvious what is mistaken about the assumption that 'freedom' of the will, however it is understood, is identical with the 'irrationality' of action. The characteristic of 'unpredictability' – equal to but not greater than the unpredictability' of 'blind, natural forces' – is the privilege of the insane. On the contrary, we associate the strongest empirical 'feeling of freedom' with precisely those actions which we know ourselves to have accomplished rationally, i.e. in the absence of physical or psychic 'compulsion'; actions in which we 'pursue' a clearly conscious 'purpose' by what to our knowledge are the most adequate 'means'.[59]

Rationality thus goes together with the freedom of action in that it is freedom itself in the form of a 'teleological' rationality:[60] the pursuit of a purpose defined by ultimate values or 'life-meanings' through the free consideration of adequate means. Such purposive-rational action concretely expresses the 'personality' as a constant relation of a human being to ultimate values. To act as a free person therefore means to act purposively, by rationally matching the available means to a defined purpose and to that extent to act logically or 'consistently'. The deliberate calculation of the opportunities for and consequences of purposively oriented action, conditioned by the means available in each case, manifests at the same time both the rationality and the freedom of the action. The freer a person is in his or her consideration and calculation of what is required (the means) for something (a particular purpose), the more his or her action assumes a purposive-rational character and thus becomes proportionally more understandable. Free action, however, is all the more closely bound to have recourse to specific appropriate means. (Or, when no such means are available, sometimes to abandon the aim itself!)

> It is precisely the person who is empirically 'free' – the person acting after deliberation – who is teleologically bound by the means for the attainment of his or her purpose. Yet these means vary according to the objective situation. The manufacturer engaged in competitive struggle and the speculator at the stock exchange gain little from their belief in their 'free will'. They face the choice between economic ruin or obedience to certain narrow maxims of economic behaviour. If they fail to obey these maxims, to their obvious loss, we will, in seeking an explanation, perhaps consider precisely this one: that they were lacking in 'will-power'. It is precisely the 'laws' of theoretical economics which necessarily presuppose the existence of 'free will' in every sense of the word which is possible in the empirical realm.[61]

The freedom to bind oneself in the pursuit of one's ultimate aims to the available means signifies nothing more nor less than the responsibility of human action. But knowledge of means – though only of means and not of purposes – is provided by rational 'science'.[62] It thus renders feasible the inner 'consistency and therefore [!] integrity' of our purposive conduct – theoretical as well as practical. The rational weighing of available means in relation to an aim which one has chosen oneself, and the weighing of the aim itself in terms of the chances and consequences of its attainment, constitute the responsibility of free, rational action. The ethical 'tension' between means and goals (i.e. that the attainment of a 'good' purpose may depend on the use of questionable means) transforms the rationality of responsibility itself into a definite ethos.

Weber contrasts this ethic of responsibility with the 'ethic of conviction', which he regards as an ethic of 'irrational' conduct because of its indifference to 'consequences'; in comparison to purposive-rational action, the ethic of conviction has a 'value-rational' orientation. The ethic of responsibility, by contrast, takes account of the prospects and consequences of action on the basis of the available means.[63] It is a relative, not an absolute, ethic because it is related to the knowledge, attained through this weighing of means, of the prospects and consequences of pursuing one's aims. If one opts for the ethic of responsibility one also decides in favour of rationality as means – ends rationality.[64] This is only in seeming contradiction to the theoretically equal weight given to purposive-rational, value-rational, affectual and traditional conduct within the 'system'.[65] The real and primary reason for Weber's obvious preference for the 'purposive-rational' schema is not the fact that it affords the greatest measure of constructive understandability of human conduct, but the specific responsibility of purposive-rational action itself. In as much as rationality thus has its roots in the ethos of responsibility, it refers back to Weber's concept of 'man' (cf. the following section).

The peculiar irrationality formed within the process of rationalisation, and which is the real motive for the investigation of this process, also appears to Weber in terms of this relation between means and ends, which for him is the basis for the concepts of rationality and freedom – namely, in terms of a reversal of this relation. That which was originally a mere means (to an otherwise valuable end) becomes itself an end or an end in itself. In this way, means as ends make themselves independent and thus lose their original 'meaning' or purpose, that is, they lose their original purposive rationality oriented to man and his needs. This reversal marks the whole of modern civilisation, whose arrangements, institutions and activities are so 'rationalised' that whereas humanity once established itself within them, now it is they which enclose and determine humanity like an 'iron cage'. Human conduct, from which these institutions originally arose, must now in turn adapt to its own creation which has escaped the control of its creator.

Weber himself declared that here lies the real problem of culture – rationalisation towards the irrational – and that he and Marx agreed in the definition of this problem but differed

in its evaluation. In his 1918 lecture on socialism which, in the
political circumstances of the time, was a remarkable tribute to
the achievement of the *Communist Manifesto*, Weber presented
the so-called 'separation' of the worker (including the 'intellectual' worker) from the means of work. He summed up: 'All
this is what *socialism* conceives as the "domination of things
over men". *This really means* the domination of means over ends
(the end being the satisfaction of needs).'[66] This paradoxical
inversion – this 'tragedy of culture', as Simmel has termed it[67]
– becomes most clearly evident when it occurs in exactly the
type of activity whose innermost intention is that it be specifically rational, namely, in *economically* rational activity. And precisely here it becomes plainly apparent that, and how,
behaviour which is purely purposive-rational in intention turns
inexorably into its own opposite in the process of its rationalisation. It then gives rise to the senseless 'irrationality' of self-
sufficient and arbitrary 'conditions' which dominate human
conduct. The rational total organisation of the conditions of life
produces, of itself, the irrational arbitrary rule of the organisation.

The entire theoretical and practical work of Marx is concerned with the explanation and destruction of this general
state of affairs; Weber's work aims at understanding it. The
Marxist economic formula for this reversal is C–M–C: M–C–M.
This economic perversion is, however, for Marx as well, the
economic form of a general perversion, which consists in the
domination of 'things' over 'men', the product (of whatever
kind) over the producer.[68] Its immediate human expression
is the objectification and specialisation of man himself – the
'particular' specialist – who is divided as a human being by his
objective activity. Like any other form of specialised enterprise,
Weber saw the specialised human being as typical of a rationalised epoch, and gave this conception of humanity his ambiguous assent.

The antinomy of Weber's political science is basically that it
is just this inexorable adjustment to the rational, enterprise-
like character of all modern institutions that becomes the locus
of possible self-realisation: the cage of 'subordination' becomes
the only available space for the 'freedom of movement' which
was Weber's primary concern, both as man and as politician.
He denied the intrinsic value of all modern institutions, but

affirmed them nevertheless as the given means towards a freely chosen purpose. On the other hand, it was precisely our recognition of the subjectivity of our ultimate judgements of purpose and value, and of our ultimate decisions, that was to assure the objectivity and realism of scientific thought and political action. In consequence, Weber's position became one of permanent opposition, with the unique aim of defending the autonomous individual amidst and in the face of the individual's growing dependence on the political and economic world. The rigorous distinctions made by Weber both in the philosophy of science and in practical conduct – the separation of object and person, of objective knowledge and subjective evaluation, of officialdom and leadership, of the ethic of responsibility and the ethic of conviction – these all arise from this single fundamental conflict between freedom and rationalisation.

The inexpressible criterion by which the irrationality of the rationalised is interpreted as such is the presupposition, shared by both Marx and Weber,[69] that the primary and absolutely autonomous purpose – the ultimate purpose of all human institutions – is not the institutions themselves but man. Everything else is merely a 'means' for 'human' purposes. For example, the economic beliefs of the bourgeois stratum of society, which were originally 'religiously' motivated – in other words, by certain human needs – become 'irrational' when, emptied of their religious content, they are transformed into profane economic activity. What began as a means towards a religious end now serves other, profane purposes. Not only this, but the mode of economic behaviour has become so autonomous that, despite all its apparent rationality, it no longer has any clear relation to the needs of human beings as such. The overriding force and arbitrariness of the circumstances of life which have developed into autonomous states of affairs are then the 'irrational' – assuming that the 'rational' is defined as the independence and autonomy of man. This holds true whether one sees man's humanity within the horizon of his social existence, as Marx did, or judges it, like Weber, by the individual character of man's responsibility to himself.

Weber's viewpoint for interpreting man's humanity (by which this irrationality is measured) is not earthly 'happiness'. This can be seen indirectly from the fact that, although he repeatedly tried to demonstrate that, for example, earning money as an end in itself is totally irrational in terms of 'happiness' or 'gain' for the individual, he never said that this inversion of 'what we would call the natural state of affairs' – an inversion which to the 'open mind' appears absolutely 'senseless' – is also simply senseless in his own view! 'We' here means 'one', for it is evident that Weber's own sympathies lay with those very Puritans to whom their work in their calling and the restless activity of their 'business' had become a 'necessity of life'. This, Weber asserted, is in fact the only fitting motivation; it brings out immediately what 'from the standpoint of personal happiness' appears so irrational about this way of life.[70]

On the other hand, it is equally evident that Weber's own ethos was no longer that of a faithful Puritan. It was a completely secularised ethos, yet it could not dispense with the 'meaning' and 'interpretation' of work.[71] The idea of the duty of one's calling clearly underlies Weber's 'demands of the day': this exponent of a 'rationalised' world wanders through our lives as a mere 'ghost' of former religious belief-systems and nobody knows yet 'who will inhabit that cage in the future'.[72] This raises the question of Weber's own attitude towards the irrational fact of universal rationalisation, whose human expression is the specialised professional. He clearly neither condemned rationalisation in Marxist terms, from the perspective of happiness, as 'inhumanity', nor affirmed it as a stage in the progress of humanity. Why did he not, like Marx, fight against this universal 'self-estrangement' of man? Why did he not, like Marx, describe this 'same' phenomenon as a 'depraved materialism' of self-alienation rather than use the scientifically neutral concept of 'rationality', which is ambiguous in its possible evaluative connotations? 'Rationality' is ambiguous because it expresses the specific achievement of the modern world and at the same time the questionable character of this achievement. Did not Weber, thus, in the same breath, both acclaim and decry this fateful process of rationalisation?[73]

He called nothing more sharply in question, with all the passion of his personality, than precisely the planned and calculated 'order', 'security' and 'specialisation' of modern life in all its political, social, economic and scientific institutions. And yet he confessed himself to be, from the first sentence of his *Sociology of Religion* to his last lecture on Science as a Vocation, a 'child of his time', a 'specialist' both as man and as scientist.[74] How could he deliberately place himself within this world, actually making himself the advocate of this 'devil' of intellectual rationalisation, and of 'the flowers of evil'? Or does his quotation of *Les fleurs du mal* allegorically reveal the secret of his own attitude to all this, and thus to the irrational rationality of our world?[75] 'If we know anything at all, we know this again today: something can be holy not only in spite of not being beautiful, but because and in as much as it is not beautiful.' He supported this observation with references to the Bible – and to Nietzsche. And he posited as 'common knowledge' that 'something can be true, although and in as much as it is neither beautiful, nor holy, nor good'.[76] Elsewhere he referred to this as 'the ethical irrationality of the world', which is unbearable for someone who espouses an absolute 'ethic of conviction'. If it were true that good can only come from good and that evil only produces evil, there would be no 'problems' of politics as a vocation.

What, then, are the 'flowers of evil', if this evil is 'rationality'? Here, indeed, the crack seems to open through which one must peer into the inner unity of this ambivalent attitude to the 'reality' which surrounds us and in which we are 'placed'. The unity of this ambivalence is the previously identified connection between rationality and freedom[77] which we must now elucidate more precisely in relation to Weber's idea of man.

This freedom can be in inner accord with rationality only if it is not a freedom from the rationalised world but a freedom within the 'iron cage', which governs even those not directly engaged in economic activity 'with overwhelming force and will perhaps continue to do so until the last hundredweight of fossil fuel has burned out'.[78] But what is the nature of this 'inner-worldly' freedom which is based on the rationalisation of our world?

RATIONALITY AS THE CAPACITY FOR INDIVIDUAL RESPONSIBILITY AMIDST UNIVERSAL DEPENDENCY

It is entirely true and confirmed by all historical experience, that the possible would not be attained unless time and again one reached out in the world for the impossible. But he who can do this must not only be a leader but also – in a very straightforward sense of the word – a hero.[79]

The positive meaning of rationality is, for Weber, its apparent opposite. This is not evident from Weber's sociology of religion, which is – in intention – a purely historical investigation. (Weber does not pursue the theme of the prophetic sentences cited in note 72 on p. 85.) Rather, it is evident from his *political* writings, particularly section II of 'Parliament and government',[80] and from a conference speech.[81] Both works fight against rationalisation in its political form as bureaucratisation and nationalisation. Weber asserts that the First World War constitutes a further advance in the process of general rationalisation, that is, in the rationally calculating, labour-dividing, specialised-bureaucratic organisation of all human institutions of authority. The process extends over the way of life of army and state as much as that of factories, scientific-technical schools and universities. Specialised examinations of all kinds increasingly become the precondition for a secure position as an official. 'This, as one knows, had been even earlier the real "Order of the Day", supported both by the interest of the universities in high enrolment and by the ambition of their students to obtain official appointments. It applies both within the state and outside it.' This prosaic fact of bureaucratic specialisation lurks even behind the 'socialism of the future'.[82] Even where socialism strives for the opposite, it ends up strengthening the power of the bureaucracy, which is the characteristic mark of the present era and the foreseeable future.

> The progressive elimination of private capitalism is theoretically quite thinkable – although this is probably not such a simple matter as some literary people, who do not know about private capitalism, dream it to be. It will certainly not be the consequence of this war. But assuming it succeeds: what would be its practical significance? The shattering of the iron cage of modern industrial work? No! Rather it would mean that the management of nationalised or in some way 'socialised' enterprises would also become bureaucratic.[83]

This 'living machine', characterised by 'rational professional specialisation and training', is exactly like an inanimate machine, 'spirit which has solidified'.

> Together with the inanimate machine, the living machine constructs the cage of future bondage. Perhaps men will be forced to fit themselves helplessly into this cage if a technically good, that is, a rational bureaucratic administration and provision of services, is to be the ultimate and the only value to decide the way in which their affairs are managed. For bureaucracy performs this task incomparably better than any other structure of domination.[84]
>
> An 'organic', that is, an oriental-Egyptian, social structure would then take shape. Yet in contrast to the oriental mood, this new social structure would be as severely rational as a machine itself. Who would deny that some such possibility lies in the womb of the future? . . . Let us assume that precisely this possibility is an inexorable fate. Who would not smile then at the fear of our literary men that future political and social development might bring too much 'individualism' or 'democracy' or suchlike, or at their assertions that 'true freedom' could dawn only when the present 'anarchy' of our economic production and the 'party games' of our parliament have been eliminated in favour of 'social order' and 'organic structure' – that is, the pacifism of social impotence under the wings of the only certainly inescapable power: bureaucracy in the state and the economy! In view of the basic fact of the irresistible advance of bureaucratisation, the question of future forms of political organisation can be posed only as follows: (1) Given this overwhelming tendency towards bureaucratisation, how is it still at all possible in any sense to preserve *any* remnants of an 'individualistic' freedom of movement?[85]

Eight years earlier (in 1909) Weber had already employed almost the same terms against the apologists for rationalisation in the area of administration and politics, though he himself was convinced that the advance of this 'human machine' was 'irresistible'. Consequently, the question one may pose is not how to change anything in this development (Marx). One cannot do this. Rather, the question is what 'follows' from this development, that is, in keeping with his earlier considerations, what, given these 'means', one can consistently aim at and want in terms of ultimate values. For 'this passion even among today's students' for bureaucratisation 'leads one to despair'.

> [It is] as if, knowingly and deliberately, we actually wanted to become men who require 'order' and nothing but order, who grow nervous and cowardly if this order falters for a moment, and who become helpless if they are uprooted from their exclusive adaptation to this order. We are anyway involved in this development towards a world which knows only these men of order. The central question, therefore, is not how to support and accelerate this trend ever further, but rather what we have to oppose to this machinery in order to preserve a *remnant of humanity* from this *fragmentation of the soul*, from this absolute domination of bureaucratic ideals of life.[86]

. The conference speech ended with an ostentatiously immoralist challenge. Weber suggested that 'the expansion of private capitalism, coupled with a purely business bureaucracy, which is more readily open to corruption' seems preferable today to 'governmental direction by the highly moral and authoritarianly transfigured German officialdom'.[87]

The only question Weber admitted in the face of irresistible bureaucratic rationalisation is how it is still at all possible, given this overpowering trend towards the rationalisation of the whole life, to preserve some remnants of some kind of 'individualistic freedom of movement'. It is this freedom of movement which Weber did not exactly 'preserve' for himself; rather, he constantly fought for it, almost for the sake of the struggle itself. A man like Jacob Burckhardt may be said to have preserved his freedom by means of a conscious withdrawal, into the 'private' sphere and into the culture of 'old Europe'.[88] A scholar of the type of E. Gothein[89] also half-preserved his freedom. But Weber, by contrast, constantly fought for this freedom, by ostentatiously and deliberately placing himself within this world, in order to oppose it from the inside by 'renunciatory action'.[90] The question, however, is how and for what? To answer this last question requires a synoptic survey of the general context of meaning in which the phenomenon of rationalisation stands.

The most general and most pervasive success of rationalisation is that which Weber has demonstrated in particular in relation to 'science' – namely, a basic disenchantment of the world.[91] The magic which surrounded the relation of man to the world in earlier epochs was, rationally expressed, the faith in some kind of 'objective' meaning. After the disenchantment of this magic, it becomes necessary to search anew for the 'meaning' of our objectivities. Hence Weber searches in particular for the meaning of science. Since all objectives have lost their objective meaning as a result of the rationalisation carried through by human beings, they are now available to human subjectivity in a new way: for the determination of their meaning. As regards the relation of man himself to the world, this disenchantment of the world which motivates the search for meaning represents a pervasive disillusionment – scientific 'open-mindedness'. The positive 'opportunity' presented by this disappointment of man and the disenchantment of the world through rationalisation is the 'sober' affirmation of everyday life and its 'demands'.[92]

This affirmation of everyday life is at the same time a denial of all forms of transcendence, including that of 'progress'. Progress then means only moving forward in the predetermined pathways of destiny, with passion and resignation. In comparison with transcendent beliefs, this belief in the destiny of the times and in the passion of temporal action is a positive absence of faith. The positive element of this lack of faith in something that goes beyond the destiny of the times and the demands of the day – this lack of faith in the objective presence of values, meanings and validities – is the subjectivity of rational responsibility as the pure responsibility of the individual towards himself. The decisive character of this individualism which Weber put in quotation marks[93] is given by the differentiation of two basically dissimilar kinds of responsibility. The specialised bureaucrat – like every rationalised specialist – is never responsible to himself as an individual but only with regard to his office: responsible to his institution and to himself as a member of that institution. In contrast to this, genuinely 'leading' politicians or 'leading' entrepreneurs – these remnants of the 'heroic age of capitalism' – act as human individuals on their own responsibility; they are therefore irresponsible precisely when they aim to make themselves responsible as an official would.[94] The basic attitude which Weber assumed in this rationalised world, and which also governed his 'methodology', is therefore the objectively unsupported obligation of the individual to himself. Placed into this world of submission, the individual, *qua* 'human being', belongs to himself and relies on himself.

The precondition for this position is precisely the world of 'ordinances', institutions, enterprises and securities to which it is opposed. Weber's own position is essentially one of opposition; his opponent is part of himself. To accomplish within the world but against it, one's own purposes which are of this world but calculated for it – this is the positive meaning of the 'freedom of movement' with which Weber was concerned. The crude political formula for Weber's basic movement of opposition is 'leadership-democracy' with a 'machine', as against both leaderless democracy and a leadership which has nothing to lead because it eschews the 'machine'. This definitive affirmation of the productivity of contradiction puts Weber in extreme opposition to Marx, who remained a Hegelian not least in his wish fundamentally to resolve the 'contradictions' in bourgeois society. And Marx, unlike Hegel, did not want merely to preserve the contradictions within the absolute organisation of the state; he wanted to eliminate them altogether in a completely non-contradictory society. The motive force of Weber's whole approach, on the other hand, was the contradiction, always conquered anew, between the recognition of a rationalised world and the counter-tendency towards freedom for self-responsibility.

The immediate human expression of this fundamental contradiction is the conflict within the human being between man and man-as-specialist. The unity of freedom and rationality therefore manifests itself most strikingly in the peculiar attitude which Weber the man assumed towards his own nature as a specialist. Here, too, the unity and divergence of his specialised interests corresponds to the unity of a human contradiction. On no occasion did Weber present himself as a totality, but merely as belonging to one or another particular sphere in this or that role, as this or that person, 'as the empirical scientific specialist in his writings, as the academic teacher in the lecture hall, as the party politician on the rostrum, and as *homo religiosus* in his intimate circle'.[95] It is precisely in this separation of various spheres of life, the theoretical expression of which is 'value-freedom', that Weber's individuality reveals itself in its unique wholeness.

Here, too, the problem for Weber was not the same as for Marx. Marx wanted to find a way to abolish the specific human existence (i.e. existence as a specialist) characteristic of the rationalised world, and also to abolish the division of labour itself. Weber asked rather how man as such, within his inevitably 'fragmented' human existence, could nevertheless preserve the freedom for the self-responsibility of the individual. And even here, Weber fundamentally affirms what Marx describes as a self-alienated humanity because, for him, precisely this form of existence did not merely permit the maximum 'freedom of movement' but enforced it. Amidst this trained and specialised world of 'specialists without spirit and hedonists without heart' one may take action here and there, with the passionate force of negativity, to break through some particular cage of 'bondage'. That was the meaning of 'freedom of movement'.

Just as Weber, in the realm of politics, posited the truly 'leading' politician and entrepreneur – the individual – as one who acts within the inevitable bureaucratisation, so he conceived the preservation of the human individual in general as taking place within a sphere of entrenched specialisation and in relation to this. In submitting to this destiny, he also set himself against it. But this opposition is based on the permanent precondition of a prior submission. Similarly, Weber's defence of so-called anarchy in economic production corresponds in purely human terms to the defence of the rights of every individuality[96] as such – of 'the last human hero'. And yet, Weber was neither an anarchist nor, in the usual sense, an individualist. He wanted to rescue the 'soul' from the overwhelming power of the 'man of order', but this 'soul' is not the sentimental soul of Rathenau's *Zur Mechanik des Geistes* (Mechanics of the Spirit). Rather it is the soul in the midst of the heartlessness of human calculation.[97]

Thus the individual, which concerned him as what is human, did not represent it for Weber an indivisible totality above or outside the particular actual mode of existence of modern specialised humanity. The individual is a 'human being' when he engages himself fully in his various separate roles, whatever is at issue and whether it is important or trivial.[98] This concept of individuality enabled Weber to commit himself to everything and nothing, to enter each situation and rely entirely on himself. This individualism, in which his idea of man is summed up, may not be capable of breaking the cage of universal affiliation and submission, yet it can break it for each person. Weber deliberately renounced the aspiration to 'universal humanity', limiting himself to the specialised work of the specialist, which he regarded as being 'in today's world the precondition for any kind of worthwhile action'. Hence this renunciation of 'total humanity' entails the stringent demand that one should engage oneself fully, despite this 'fragmentation of the soul', by the passion of each – in itself – fragmented action. 'For nothing has any value for man as a man, unless it can be done with passion.'[99]

This 'demon' of his passion could also be called the idol of a humanity deprived of its gods. With this as the groundless ground of his purposes, and amidst his own efforts towards scientific and political objectivity, Weber fought against the belief in objectively worthwhile aims, institutions and concepts as a form of idolatry and superstition. All this in order to preserve the human hero. In this, remarks Honigsheim, he was ultimately helped by the sociological method of destroying all absolute value claims made by the representatives of institutions. 'Sociology' was of particular use in the service of this freedom of movement. By this method, Weber created for himself a 'platform of negativity' on which the human hero – 'in a very modest sense of the word' – could develop his activity.[100] The intellectual expression of this humanity Weber called 'plain intellectual integrity'. It consists in giving 'account' to oneself 'of the ultimate meaning of one's own actions'.[101]

This idea of human freedom does not contrast merely with the average individualism, which Hegel and Marx opposed as the philistine freedom of private whim. It also stands in extreme contrast to the kind of 'freedom' to which Marx wanted 'humanly' to emancipate humanity, and which, to him, was the freedom of the 'highest community'. This Marxian idea Weber regarded as utopian. Conversely, Marx would have considered Weber's human hero as 'calling up from the dead' the heroic times of the bourgeoisie, whose 'sober reality' is 'unheroic' and merely the 'ghost' of its great epoch.[102] What was for Weber an 'unavoidable destiny' was for Marx merely the 'prehistory' of humanity. Where Marx put the beginning of true human history, there Weber saw the beginning of an ethic of irresponsible 'conviction'. This difference in their view of the world and their idea of humanity is expressed in the dissimilarity of their determining perspectives for the interpretation of the modern bourgeois-capitalist world. For Weber: 'rationality'. For Marx: 'alienation'.

NOTES

1 Friedrich Gundolf, 1880–1930. German historian of literature, member of the 'George Circle' (cf. Chapter 1, note 16). This is part of a poem addressed to Max Weber (cf. Gundolf, *Gedichte*, pp. 23 ff.) [Eds].

2 ' "Objectivity" in social science and social policy', in Shils and Finch, 1949, p. 72. Landshut, 1929, pp. 13 ff., has pointed out that even the sentences immediately following this, which contain a theoretical determination of 'reality', are at variance. We shall not further examine the objective unsuitability of Weber's 'conceptual apparatus' because we – unlike Landshut – consider it inappropriate to evaluate Weber's 'problematic' in terms of Marxian theoretical precepts and categories. Our intention is to depict the independent quality of his guiding principle for the interpretation of capitalism in its original difference from that of Marx – regardless of the questionable nature of Weber's methodology and conceptual categorisation.

3 This is a reference to the slogan, coined by the German historian Leopold von Ranke (1795–1886), that the job of the historian is to find out 'how it actually was', *wie es eigentlich gewesen ist* [Eds].

4 cf. Freyer, 1930, pp. 156 ff.

5 ' "Objectivity" in social science and social policy', in Shils and Finch, 1949, p. 76.

6 ibid., p. 78.

7 ibid., p. 64.

8 ibid., p. 76.

9 Exceptions which confirm this general characterisation are Korsch, particularly *Marxism and Philosophy*, pp. 73 ff., and Lukács, 1923, pp. 103 ff. and pp. 181 ff.

10 cf. particularly 'Science as a vocation', in Gerth and Mills, 1947, especially pp. 132, 138 ff. and 152 ff.; also Weber, 1924b, p. 252; 1904a, pp. 15 ff.; 1903–6, pp. 115 ff.; and ' "Objectivity" in social science and social policy', in Shils and Finch, 1949.

11 cf. Honigsheim, 1968, pp. 132 ff.

12 Nietzsche, 1887, third essay: 'What do ascetic ideals mean?'

13 ' "Objectivity" in social science and social policy', in Shils and Finch, 1949, p. 110.

14 ibid.

15 ibid. On the meaning of the thesis of 'value freedom', cf. Honigs-heim, 1968, pp. 128 ff.; Freyer, 1930, pp. 208 ff.; and Siegfried Landshut, 'Max Webers geistesgeschichtliche Bedeutung', *Neue Jahrbücher für Wissenschaft und Jugenbildung*, vol. 6, 1931.

16 Shils and Finch, 1949, p. 60.

17 ibid., p. 52.

18 ibid., p. 54.

19 loc. cit.

20 loc. cit.

21 ibid., p. 57.

22 The presupposition here expressed, that of (bourgeois-capitalist) 'society', as something distinct from all earlier structures of *gemeinschaftlich* social life, is something which Weber's sociology shares with the problematic and the origins of modern sociology in general (from Hegel, via Stein, to Marx). On this, see E. Fech-ner, 'Der Begriff des kapitalistischen Geistes bei W. Sombart and M. Weber und die soziologischen Grundkategorien Gemeinschaft und Gesellschaft', *Weltwirtschaftliches Archiv*, October 1929. Even Weber's first investigation of occidental capitalism, 'Die Börse' (the stock exchange), viewed the stock exchange as a symbol indicating dissolution of community (*Gemeinschaft*) into society (*Gesellschaft*). Compare Weber's position in regard to Tönnies in *Economy and Society*, Vol. 1, pp. 40 ff. See also note 77 below, on H. J. Grab's criticism of Weber.

23 Honigsheim, 1968, p. 131.

24 'Critical studies in the logic of the cultural sciences', in Shils and Finch, 1949, p. 163, n. 30; and Weber, 1903–6, p. 238, n. 11.

25 On this concept of atheism, cf. Löwith, 1964, pp. 368 ff. [Eds].

26 'Science as a vocation', in Gerth and Mills, 1947, p. 149.

27 ' "Objectivity" in social science and social policy', in Shils and Finch, 1949, p. 112.

28 'Critical studies in the logic of the cultural sciences', in ibid., p. 116.

29 Weber presumably derived this expression from Lask's character-isation of Hegel's Logic. Emil Lask, 1875–1915; cf. Lask, 1902, esp. pp. 25 ff., 56–67 [Eds].

30 One may already observe here the decisive importance for Weber of 'consistency' as the expression of every 'responsible' position; cf. the following chapter.

31 Weber, 1903–6, pp. 90 ff.

32 ibid., pp. 111, 116 ff. ' "Objectivity" in social science and social policy', in Shils and Finch, 1949, pp. 58, 60.

33 Weber, 1903–6, p. 88.

34 ibid., p. 199.

35 ibid., p. 205.

36 In order to master this relationship conceptually, Weber created for himself the construct of the 'ideal-type', the basic philosophical character of which lies in the fact that it lays open reality while at the same time constructing it. Landshut in 'Max Weber's

geistesgeschichtliche Bedeutung' (pp. 38 ff.), sees in the artificiality of this construction an abandonment of Weber's own investigative aim to attain a knowledge of reality in its own meaning – 'a lack of relation between value orientation and reality', based more generally on an erroneous 'disjunction between humanity and the world'. What Landshut fails to see is that man's ontological 'existence' as being-in-the-world (Heidegger) does not in itself imply anything concerning the anthropologically determinate mode of this ontological unity. The historical specificity of modern 'being-in-the-world' is characterised for Weber and Marx by 'rationalisation' and 'self-alienation'. This is what produces the 'disjunction' of man and world, to which corresponds the more or less 'constructivist' character of all modern conceptualisation and the technical character of its practice. According to Lukács's insight, this socio-historically created dualism is also the cause of the dualistic conceptual structure of all modern philosophy and its antinomies (Lukács, 1923, pp. 110 ff.). Lewalter ('Wissenssoziologie und Marxismus', *Archiv für Sozialwissenschaft und Sozialpolitik*, vol. 64, 1930), who criticises Lukács for his 'logicist' interpretation of Marx, misapprehends, in my view, the positive significance of this approach, which lies in the fact that Lukács – consistently following Marx – provides a socio-historical interpretation of even the most abstract categories of philosophy and thus reveals their specificity (cf. preface to Marx, *Contribution to the Critique of Political Economy*), while at the same time he outlines the possibility of a revolution even at the theoretical level, accompanying the revolution in the foundations of the entire human-social mode of existence. Concerning the concept of the ideal-type, see also Alexander von Schelting's essay in the *Archiv für Sozialwissenschaft und Sozialpolitik*, vol. 49, 1922. [Compare von Schelting, 1934. Eds.]

37 Dilthey, 1959, Vol. 1, pp. 351 ff.

38 cf. Weber's characterisation of this state in 'Bureaucracy and political leadership', in *Economy and Society*, Vol. III, pp. 1393 ff.

39 cf. Hegel, 1821, para. 183 [Eds].

40 See Marx, 'Critique of Hegel's Philosophy of the State', especially the sections referring to paras 279 and 303; see also pp. 102–9 below [Eds].

41 See Weber, 1921b, Vol. I, pp. 13 ff.; and Spann, 1914, pp. 317 ff.

42 When Freyer (1930, p. 177) says that Weber's methodological individualism often changes to a substantive individualism in spite of his intentions, one may ask whether this does not in itself arise from a theoretical inversion of the really decisive relationship. Freyer himself demands the formation of concepts which account for both the objective formedness and the human vividness of social phenomena. But even this 'double perspective' cannot escape the question where the real accent of our social, and hence of our sociological, problematic is located, especially since, in Freyer's own view, sociology is itself socio-historically rooted.

Freyer's own distinction between social reality and the constructs of 'objective spirit' presupposes a specific non-binding attachment of man – namely, modern man – to the social 'order'; in general terms, a structure of 'society' rather than 'community'. On this point, cf. Grab, 1927, p. 23. Grab, too, misunderstands the social philosophical meaning of Weber's sociological 'individualism' when he sees it merely as an 'absolutisation' of one specific 'sphere' of reality to the whole of reality.

43 ' "Objectivity" in social science and social policy', in Shils and Finch, 1949, pp. 101 ff.

44 Weber, 1903–6, p. 229, n. 81.

45 That the freedom of the individual is only 'apparently' the opposite of rationalisation should not imply that the general success of rationalisation is not after all the unfreedom of the individual; cf. 'Bureaucracy and political leadership', in Weber, 1921b, Vol. III, p. 1394. The question is what 'value' this had for Weber himself.

46 'Science as a vocation', in Gerth and Mills, 1947, p. 155.

47 Weber, 1904a, p. 193, n. 9.

48 Freyer, 1930, p. 157.

49 Weber, 1920, Vol. I, p. 537. The only attempt so far to clarify Weber's concept of 'rationality' in its original conceptual nexus and in relation to Marx has been made by Landshut ('Max Webers geistesgeschichtliche Bedeutung', pp. 54 ff. and pp. 77 ff.). Landshut tries to prove that the distinction between 'rational' and 'irrational' was derived from economic behaviour as the specifically 'rational' form of behaviour. The original source of this basic distinction is therefore capitalism. Capitalism, according to Landshut, is the 'original' from which Weber initially derived the concept of rationality, and hence it also constitutes the thematic identity between Weber and Marx. But whereas Marx progresses from here to the analysis of the capitalist process of production as the 'anatomy' of bourgeois society, Weber's interpretation of the same phenomenon in terms of sociology of religion tends towards a critique of the Marxian account. Instead of inquiring into the basis of this divergence, Landshut attempts to prove that while Weber accepted Marx's formulation of the problem and his categorisation of reality (in terms of 'factors'), he did not accept the associated practical aim of human emancipation through transformation of the world. Landshut's reflections in this regard are informative for our inquiry and they touch on the central sociological problem. Yet they do not approach the really characteristic motive in Weber's work anywhere near as closely as they do in explicating Marx in terms of his dominant motive. Landshut expresses this himself when he says in regard to his presentation of Weber that he is aware 'that the connection with economic theory is in no way exhaustive and that even the original basis of Weber's thought is not to be sought primarily in the realm of economics'. At the same time, Landshut precludes the possibility

of analysing Weber by measuring Weber's formulation of the problem against the practically less ambiguous and hence more transparent problem-formulation in Marx. As a result, he fails to see the positive meaning just in the absence of an analogous 'structure' in Weber's sociology (see the following chapter and also Chapter 4).

50 Introduction to *Religionssoziologie*, Vol. I, in Gerth and Mills, 1947, p. 267.
51 Weber, 1904a, pp. 47 ff., 52.
52 cf. Marx's opposed comment on Bastiat, *Capital*, Vol. I, ch. 1.
53 Weber, 1921c.
54 Weber, 1903–6, pp. 97 ff.
55 Wach, in his presentation of Weber's sociology of religion (Wach, 1931, pp. 79 ff.), also notes that this passage is 'characteristic' for Weber but leaves entirely unexplained to what extent it is characteristic. Wach regrets that Weber's death did not 'allow' him to provide for this enormously 'important historical statement a strictly organised and systematic development of the basic categories of the domain of the sociology of religion'. But he never asks himself whether Weber's investigations within the sociology of religion, which were directed towards the sociology of rationalisation in general, can be evaluated in terms of a separate discipline – the 'sociology of religion' – with a definable 'object domain' and particular 'objects of investigation'. Actually it is only Wach, and not Weber, who is interested in the precise delimitation and isolation from 'neighbouring' problematics of 'themes which, formally at least, unquestionably belong to the sociology of religion'. By way of contrast, cf. Freyer, 1930, pp. 146 ff.
56 Weber, 1903–6, pp. 120 ff.
57 ibid.
58 ibid., pp. 191 ff.; cf. pp. 127 ff., 198.
59 'Critical studies in the logic of the cultural sciences', in Shils and Finch, 1949, pp. 124 ff.
60 See Gerth and Mills, 1947, p. 324, where rationality is also conceived as a rationality of the teleological 'consistency' of theoretical or practical behaviour.
61 Weber, 1903–6, pp. 193–4.
62 ' "Objectivity" in social science and social policy', in Shils and Finch, 1949, p. 53; and 'Science as a vocation', in Gerth and Mills, 1947, p. 151.
63 'Politics as a vocation', in Gerth and Mills, 1947, pp. 122 ff. and pp. 125 ff.
64 See E. Voegelin, 'Max Weber', *Deutsche Vierteljahresschrift für Literaturwissenschaft und Geistesgeschichte*, Vol. 3, 1925, pp. 180 ff.
65 Weber, 1921b, Vol. I, pp. 22 ff.; cf. the critique by Grab, 1927, p. 33; Landshut, 'Max Webers geistesgeschichtliche Bedeutung' and A. Walther, *Jahrbuch für Soziologie*, 1926, pp. 62 ff. In fact,

even in this theoretical juxtaposition there is an emphasis on expressed purposive rationality.

66 *Gesammelte Aufsätze zur Soziologie und Sozialpolitik.* [In W. G. Runciman, 1978, p. 253; emphasis Löwith's. Eds.]

67 Simmel extended this historical inversion into an absolute philosophical principle, transforming the tragedy of our 'culture' into a 'turning' of life in general towards the 'idea' – an immanent 'transcendence of life'; cf. Lukács, 1923, pp. 94 ff., pp. 156 ff. [See also Simmel, 1968. Eds]

68 *Capital,* Vol. I, ch. 4.

69 Weber, 1904a, pp. 53 ff., 70, 78.

70 See P. Honigsheim, 'Max Webers geistesgeschichtliche Stellung' (in Honigsheim, 1968), on the 'characteristic unhappiness of the scientific man', such as Max Weber.

71 See Weber, 1904a, p. 182.

72 'Nobody knows yet who will inhabit that cage in the future and whether, at the end of this tremendous development, there will be entirely new prophets or a powerful rebirth of old thoughts and ideals; or, if neither of these, whether there will be mechanised petrification, embellished by a kind of rigid self-importance. In that case it would indeed become true of the "last men" of such a cultural development; "specialists without spirit, hedonists without heart; this nonentity maintains the illusion that it has reached a stage of humanity never before attained" ' (ibid.).

73 See Freyer, 1930, pp. 157–8, who points to the ambiguity of Weber's evaluation of the rationalisation process, but does not further elucidate this ambiguity.

74 Weber explicitly leaves the evaluation of his sociology of religion to 'specialists', and, for example, not to philosophers (whom he regarded however as equally specialists!).

75 'Science as a vocation', in Gerth and Mills, 1947, pp. 147–8; 'Politics as a vocation', in ibid., pp. 121 ff.

76 ibid.

77 H. J. Grab, in an inquiry into the concept of the rational in Max Weber's sociology (1927), has tried to answer the following question: what values constitute rationality for Weber? Eventually he also hits upon the freedom of the responsible individual. But Weber had already more or less dealt with the problem of historical value-relativism, for he concluded, according to Grab, from the lack of generally binding communities and values, that what is subjectively binding is one's own decision to uphold ultimate values. 'Only the pathos of this conviction allows us to suspect how in Weber's mind everything converges with magnificent consistency into a unified world-image. This philosophy of history leads us to understand that sociology aims merely at being a science of *Verstehen* (understanding) and has nothing to say about objective connections. From this we understand the fact of value-free science, the separation of reality and value' (p. 42). However, this insight does not lead Grab to penetrate into

Weber's sociology, because for Grab himself, the values of the 'rational' are *eo ipso* 'lower' and 'subaltern' values referring to the sphere of the merely biological and the merely utilitarian – absolutised products of 'technical' intelligence, of the mere process of civilisation and the mechanical science of nature which corresponds to it. Grab adheres to Scheler's doctrine – diametrically opposed to Weber's position – which posits an evident, objective hierarchy of a fixed set of values. Consequently he sees in Weber's position only a sanctioning of a 'transvaluation of values', an inversion of the 'natural' order of values. He counters this with the 'possible (!) restoration of the true order of values', which is not 'historically subjected' to the actually predominant spirit of the time but arises from the 'correct evaluation' of the goods of civilisation. 'One may not ask here whether there is a chance today for the restoration of the value order in all spheres of our life or whether sociology can merely aim at bringing us back in our minds to the idea of a natural social order and to uphold such an idea through time' (pp. 45–6).

But this is precisely the question which should have been asked here, for this forms the basis not merely of Grab's critique but also of his characterisation of Weber. Without deciding this question, it is not Weber's position which remains a 'historical' issue and a 'withdrawal from the world', but rather the position of his critics. This remains so even if those critics do not associate themselves with Kahler's critique of the 'old' science of Weber. The idea of 'rational' science as Weber understood it is no more obsolete than Nietzsche's 'scientific atheism' within the realm of philosophy, which in *The Will to Power* made it clear that 'European nihilism' was the consequence of precisely the objective value-interpretation of existence. According to Nietzsche, 'one no longer has any grounds to persuade oneself of a "true" world'; rather, the categories with which we had previously imposed an objective meaning and value on the world must now be taken back again from the 'world' and related back to man. The world then seems 'valueless' at first, but only because one has not yet devalued those categories (Nietzsche, 1901, book I, section 1). Weber's interpretation of values must also be understood on this level, marked out by Nietzsche, in which our previous values are called into question. The 'way out', the 'contradiction' and the 'conflict' are not in Weber but in Scheler, to whose material value-ethic Grab appeals and with whom he 'conceives' the phenomenon of 'value' as a palpable 'Ur-phenomenon' (p. 12). Constrained by this orientation to Scheler, Grab's instructive analyses stop at the penultimate stage and he is prevented from really carrying out his intention: to reduce Weber's individual theses to their 'ultimate philosophical grounds'.

78 Weber, 1904a, p. 181.
79 'Politics as a vocation', in Gerth and Mills, 1947, p. 128.

80 'Parliament and government in a reconstructed Germany', in Weber, 1921b, Vol. III, p. 1381 ff.
81 Weber, 1924a, pp. 412 ff. This is a contribution to a discussion in the *Verein für Sozialpolitik* (Vienna, 1909) on the economic activities of local government [Eds].
82 Weber, 1924b, pp. 253 ff; and 'Politics as a vocation', in Gerth and Mills, 1947, pp. 99 ff., in regard to Russia.
83 'Bureaucracy and political leadership', in Weber, 1921b, Vol. III, pp. 1401 ff.
84 ibid., p. 1402.
85 ibid., pp. 1402 ff.
86 'Economic activities of local government', in Weber, 1924a, pp. 412 ff. [The two last phrases were italicised by Löwith. Eds.]
87 ibid.
88 See the letters of Jacob Burckhardt (1955). [Jacob Burckhardt, 1818–1897, Swiss historian of culture. Author of *The Civilisation of the Renaissance in Italy* (1860). Eds.]
89 It is highly significant which types of religious existence were secularised by Burckhardt, Gothein and Weber. Burckhardt secularised the 'anchorites' of the period of decline of the ancient world, Gothein drew comfort from the neo-Platonic philosophy of Boethius, and Weber found an interpretation of himself in the ancient Jewish prophets. [Eberhard Gothein, 1853–1923, German cultural historian and economist. Eds.]
90 Weber, 1904a, pp. 180 ff.
91 'Science as a vocation', in Gerth and Mills, 1947, p. 139.
92 On this point and in regard to what follows see the general characterisation of Max Weber by Voegelin, Honigsheim and Landshut in their previously cited works; with particular regard to Stefan George, see Wolters, 1930, bk 6, ch. 5, pp. 470 ff.
93 This individualism of Weber is evident even in his style; in his excessive use of quotation marks. Someone who puts common words within quotes thereby designates them as 'so-called', meaning that they are generally used in this way by others. This implies that I use them only in a distanced way, with reservations or, more directly: really with another meaning of my own.
94 Weber, 1921b, Vol. III, p. 1404; Gerth and Mills, 1947, p. 45.
95 Honigsheim, 1968, p. 125; only in Franciscan nominalism does Honigsheim find anything analogous to this.
96 See 'Der Max-Weber-Kreis in Heidelberg', in ibid., pp. 271 ff.
97 In his philosophical novel *The Man without Qualities* Robert Musil has given a psychological interpretation of this problem of the age.
98 Compare Karl Jasper's (1921) emphasis on the 'fragmentary' character of Weber's entire activity.
99 'Science as a vocation', in Gerth and Mills, 1947, p. 135.
100 Honigsheim, 1968, p. 133.
101 In the realm of philosophy, this reduction of scientific truth to 'intellectual integrity' corresponds to Nietzsche's reduction of

Truth *in toto* to 'honesty' as the 'ultimate virtue' of 'free, self-possessed' minds. See *Beyond Good and Evil*, section 7 ('Our virtues'), para. 227; *The Genealogy of Morals*, third essay ('Ascetic ideals'), paras 24 and 27; *Human, All Too Human*, Vol. 2, 'The wanderer and his shadow', paras 212 ff.

102 Marx, *The Eighteenth Brumaire of Louis Bonaparte*, section 1.

Chapter 3

Marx's interpretation of the bourgeois-capitalist world in terms of human 'self-alienation'

THE HISTORICAL DEVELOPMENT OF THE CONCEPT FROM HEGEL THROUGH FEUERBACH TO MARX

The specifically 'Marxist' theme in the analysis of the bourgeois-capitalist world is not its self-alienation, but its 'anatomy', its skeletal structure – that is to say, its political economy – a term which grasps economic existence and consciousness in a dialectical unity. At first glance, the emphasis on the anatomy of bourgeois society signifies no more than a change of emphasis from 'bourgeois society' in Hegel's sense to the 'system of needs' as such. It depicts the material relations of production as the skeletal structure of this society. At the same time, this approach also includes the much broader and more questionable thesis of the fundamental importance of the material conditions of life as the determinant of all other aspects, which eventually crystallises in the vulgar Marxist thesis of so-called 'real base' as the foundation on which there arises a superstructure that is to be interpreted as purely ideological. It is in this form, which is not merely vulgarised but disfigured, that Marxism has generally become the object of both criticism and defence. This is how Weber also regarded Marxism and combated it as a dogmatically economistic historical materialism.

Leaving aside the question of how far Marx himself, and even more Engels, gave support to this vulgar Marxist conception, the fact remains that after Marx had achieved self-clarification in philosophy the critique of political economy became his primary concern. 'Marx's development in this respect can be summarised in the brief formula: he undertook first a philosophical critique of religion, then a political critique of religion, philosophy, politics and all other ideologies.'[1] Yet the specifically economic interpretation of all manifestations of human life is, according to Marx himself, only the final result of his critical revision of the Hegelian philosophy of right – and Hegel considered a 'result' as 'the corpse which the vital impulse has left behind'. This vital impulse in the result – the critique of self-alienation – is what will be brought to light from Marx's early writings in the following discussion. The principal sources for this purpose are the writings of 1841–5, and I shall interpret these in turn with particular reference to Weber's guiding principle of rationalisation. This thematic limitation does not imply that the young Marx can be completely separated from the mature Marx, and the latter handed over to the 'Marxists' while the former is assigned to bourgeois philosophy. On the contrary, Marx's early writings are and remain fundamental even for *Capital*, and if the first chapter of Volume I of *Capital* is a 'result', the vital impulse that produced it can be found already in a discussion in the *Rheinische Zeitung* of 1842.

The basic theme, for Marx as for Weber, is the encompassing reality in which we are placed; and the original form of Marx's critical analysis of the capitalist process of production is a critique of the bourgeois world as a whole in terms of its human self-alienation. This bourgeois-capitalist world represents for Marx, as a Hegelian, 'ir-rational' reality, a human world which is inhuman, a perverted human world. And just as Weber found it necessary to understand the 'demon' of rationalisation, to 'trace its course to the end in order to grasp its strength and limits', so Marx also declared that it is important to study 'this master of the world'. In the preface to his doctoral dissertation, and in a letter to Ruge (1843), Mark called himself an 'idealist' who had the insolent desire to 'turn human beings into genuinely human beings'.[2] What we have to show first is that Marx was concerned throughout with human beings as such, even when he thought he had discovered the possibility of a 'new' man in the proletariat. His ultimate aim was and remained 'a human emancipation of humanity', a 'real humanism'. The historical connection of this basic orientation with Rousseau is unmistakable.[3]

In the German philosophy of the time this concentration upon the human being as such was the underlying tendency of Feuerbach's transformation of pure philosophy into philosophical anthropology. The philosophy which he regarded as the ultimate form of an absolute philosophy was Hegel's philosophy of absolute spirit. From this starting point both Feuerbach and Marx concentrated their critical philosophy upon the human being as such, who does not play a leading role in Hegel's philosophy of absolute, objective and subjective, spirit. Hegel defined man as spirit (*Geist*) according to his essential 'Being' (*Encyclopaedia*, para. 377).[4] He appears as man in Hegel's *Philosophy of Right* in the guise of the subject of mundane 'needs', and Hegel conceived civil society as the system of these needs. What he called 'man' is therefore already, and merely, the member of civil society as the subject of mundane needs. Defined in this way man does not embody, for either Hegel or Marx, a genuine human universality. He is a mere particularity, for Hegel in relation to the true universality of the state (which in turn is the concrete embodiment of reason), and for Marx in relation to the true universality of a classless, truly human society. Hegel made the following distinctions in the *Philosophy of Right*:

> In law, the object is the person, from a moral standpoint the subject, in the family the family-member, in civil society as a whole the citizen (as bourgeois). Here, from the perspective of needs, it is the concrete form of the representation which is called man; hence it is here and only here that we speak of man in this sense. (para. 190)

Hegel did not altogether dismiss the concept of man as such and in general. But he recognised it only with respect to civil rights, and it is precisely in this that Hegel's eminently realistic grasp of the surrounding 'reality' is shown. He says (para. 209 and note to para. 270) that every human being is first of all a human being, though differing in race, nationality, faith, status and vocation; and that his sheer humanity is by no means a 'flat, abstract' quality. But Hegel saw the true significance of this universal quality in the fact that 'there emerges as a consequence of the granting of civil rights . . . the self-awareness of counting as a *juridical* person in *civil society*'. And this – this humanity validated by civil rights – Hegel argued, is the 'infinite and independent root' from which there emerges also 'the desired adjustment of the mode of thought and sentiments'.

Hegel explicitly resisted giving this definition (of man simply as man) an absolute character. For even if all individuals are equal in so far as they are considered only as 'human beings' (and not as Italians or Germans, Catholics or Protestants), this self-consciousness – the consciousness of being nothing more than a human being – would be 'inadequate', if it established itself ('perhaps as cosmopolitan politics') in opposition to the public life of the state as something which has its own specific, fundamental and autonomous significance.[5] In Hegel's *Philosophy of Spirit*, therefore, the essential character of the human species is not that man is in some sense 'human' but that he is a 'spiritual' being.[6] Hence Hegel's discussion of 'alienation' is fundamentally different from that of Feuerbach and Marx, even though the structural form of the 'category' is the same. Hegel subordinated to this specifically ontological definition of man (as 'spirit') the conception of man as the subject of civil rights and mundane needs; and it is only man characterised in this way (of whom only a 'representation' but not a genuine philosophical concept can be formed) that he called man. It is evident that Hegel believed more strongly in the spirituality of man than in his humanity.

Feuerbach's overriding aim was to transform this independent philosophy of spirit into a humanistic philosophy of man.[7] He indicated the task of his 'new' philosophy of the 'future' as follows: 'At the present time [1843] it is not a question of describing man, but of extricating him from the ['idealistic'] morass into which he has sunk.' The task was 'to develop from the philosophy of the absolute, i.e. from [philosophical] theology, the necessity of the philosophy of man, i.e. anthropology, and to found a critique of human philosophy by means of a critique of divine philosophy' (Preface to *Grundsätze der Philosophie der Zukunft*) (Principles of the Philosophy of the Future). This intention of making man the object of philosophy stems from the desire to make philosophy the object of humanity.[8]

In accordance with his anthropological principle, Feuerbach contested Hegel's particularising definition of man. Starting from the definition in the *Philosophy of Right* (cited above), where Hegel says that only in the context of civil society is it possible to speak of human beings in this sense, Feuerbach continued polemically: whether we speak of the legal 'person' or the moral 'subject' – or any other such category – in truth we refer to one and the same total human being, but in 'different senses'. For it is a characteristic quality of man that he can always be defined in a variety of ways by his role and function: as a private person, an official, a citizen, and so on. Thus Feuerbach rejected Hegel's particularising concept of man, but unlike Marx he did not take this concrete particularity seriously, did not show how this factually divided humanity of man in modern bourgeois-capitalist society (his specialisation of function) could be restored to unity; not through a Feuerbachian 'communism of love' in 'I–thou' relationships, but through the supersession of the previous forms of the division of labour, and in particular their class character.

But Marx's critique of man in bourgeois society, and hence in the modern world, is also based upon Feuerbach's anthropological perspective. In *The Holy Family* Marx still identified himself with Feuerbach's 'real humanism'. The book begins with the following sentence: 'Real humanism in Germany has no more dangerous enemy than spiritualism or speculative idealism, which posits in place of the real individual human being "self-consciousness" or "spirit", and teaches, like the gospels, that only the spirit gives life.' Similarly, Marx's critique of Hegel's *Philosophy of Right* begins with a reference to Feuerbach's reduction of theology to anthropology, for this critique is seen as a prerequisite for further criticism of man's this-worldly condition.[9] This acceptance of Feuerbach[10] corresponds with a polemic (which, however incidental, follows the same lines) against Hegel's particularising definition of man.

Marx compared man in bourgeois society with the commodity, as a product of simple labour. For like a commodity, man assumes a questionable 'double character': in economic terms a 'value form', and a 'natural form'. As a commodity – that is, as incorporated labour – something is worth a certain sum of money, and in that context its natural characteristics are more or less irrelevant. As 'commodities', various goods may have quite a different economic value, although they share the same natural characteristics. Similarly, the human being in this world of commodities, existing in its bourgeois value form, plays an important role, in his own eyes and in those of others, perhaps as 'a general or a banker', but in any case as a specialised individual, fixed and fragmented by his objective activity;

while as a 'mere' human being as such – in his natural form, so to speak – he plays only a shabby part. Here Marx refers laconically in a note to paragraph 190 of Hegel's *Philosophy of Right*. This reference can be interpreted as follows: if Hegel makes man as such so particular and partial a thing as is the subject of needs endowed with civil rights, existing alongside other equally partial determinations, this apparently purely theoretical fragmentation of man simply reflects an actual de-spiritualisation and inhumanity in the real conditions of existence of modern humanity. For there corresponds to this theoretical segregation, fixation and autonomy – this 'rationalis-ation' of man in terms of particular modes of existence – a division, fixation and autonomy which prevails in reality. This permits only partial manifestations of 'being human', in the face of what are in fact abstract concretions, which no longer address the whole man, man as such, but only man in his specialised function.

Among such concretions, which are abstract in the sense that they abstract from the totality of 'being human', are the bourgeois or proletarian class individual, man as intellectual or as manual worker, and in general the modern individual with his vocation or specialised task; but above all the universal separation of man in bourgeois society into two distinct and contradictory modes of existence: the private person with his private morality, and the public citizen with his public morality. In all these partial manifestations of human existence the whole man still appears, but not without contradiction or simply as a human being. In so far as he is defined by one or other of his particular aspects it is only by reference to some other specific character, such as having a certain vocation by implicit contrast with his family life, or as a private individual by con-trast with his public life. In all these particular independent manifestations of his humanity – as either this or that – a person is 'human' only in a conditional and limited sense, and in bourgeois society, at the most, as a so-called private individual. It is not man 'as such' who plays a fundamental part in a society so differentiated and fragmented (rationalised), but only the fixed entity, which the individual constitutes through his position and activities. Because these social posi-tions and activities are largely determined by economic conditions, by mundane 'needs', Hegel's definition of man, according to which man as such is only a particularised being, is itself, therefore, not a mere speculative construction but the appropriate theoretical expression of a real 'inhumanity' in the actual conditions of existence of the modern bourgeois-capitalist world – an indication that in this society man is alienated from himself as a human being.

Feuerbach and Marx were in agreement, therefore, in considering that Hegel's philosophy of mind treats man only as a particularised entity, not as the underlying human and philosophical totality. Yet because it is the human being as such, and as a whole, which constitutes both the starting point and the goal for Marx, he was obliged to reveal the total, subjective particularisation of man in bourgeois society, which in Hegel's philosophy of spirit is concealed as much as it is disclosed. In other words, Marx was concerned to show that the apparent obviousness with which the bourgeois society the bourgeois and the human being are equated, is a questionable assumption, not only in terms of its specific particularisms but as a whole particularistic view which bourgeois man represents. In order to liberate man from his total subjective particularity, and to overcome the human alienation resulting from specialisation, Marx called for an 'emancipation of man' which will be not only political and economic, but a 'human' emancipation. This does not relate, however, to man as 'ego and alter ego' (Feuerbach), but to the human 'world'; for man himself is his social world: he is essentially a *zoon politikon*. Hence Marx's critique of man in bourgeois society culminates in a critique of society and the economy, but without thereby losing its basic anthropological meaning.[11] Marx traced this fundamental and universal self-alienation of man in modern political, social and economic structures – that is, in the same 'order' that we encountered in Weber as the inescapable destiny of rationalisation – in all its aspects: in its economic, political and directly social forms. The economic expression of this problematic is the world of commodities; its political expression, the contradiction between the bourgeois state and bourgeois society; its direct human-social expression, the existence of the proletariat.

THE ECONOMIC EXPRESSION OF HUMAN SELF-ALIENATION IN THE COMMODITY

> As with every historical social science, it must be noted in the development of economic categories that modern bourgeois society is a 'given', whose categories therefore express forms of existence, existential determinants, which are often only isolated aspects of this specific society, and consequently that economics, *even as a science*, did not by any means begin only when it was first mentioned as such.
>
> (Marx, *Contribution to the Critique of Political Economy*)

The economic expression of human alienation is the 'commodity' as representative of the saleable character of all objects of the modern world. The commodity of Marx's sense does not signify one particular type of object among others; instead, for him the commodity embodies the basic ontological character of all our objects, their 'commodity form'. This commodity form or structure characterises the alienation both of things and of human individuality.[12] *Capital* therefore begins with an analysis of the commodity. The criticism of society, and hence the basic human significance of this economic analysis, finds direct expression in *Capital* only in the marginal comments and footnotes, but it emerges clearly in Marx's article on the debate in the Rhenish Diet on the proposed legislation against thefts of wood.[13] This article embodies the first, exemplary revelation of that fundamental inversion of 'means' and 'ends', of 'object' and 'man', which involves the alienation of man, his self-dispossession in favour of the 'thing'. To regard oneself as something 'other' and 'foreign', this supreme form of externalisation, is what Marx, in his doctoral dissertation,[14] calls 'materialism', while referring to himself as an 'idealist' who wants to overcome this alienation. The externalisation of man in favour of a thing is self-alienation, because things are essentially there for human beings while human beings are ends in themselves. What Marx wants to convey in his article is essentially the following: wood, which belongs to a proprietor and can be stolen, is not simply wood, but an object of economic and social significance, and hence of general human significance. As such an important object, wood is not the same for its possessor, a private owner, as it is for the non-owner who steals it. It is therefore impossible to devise a form of punishment that is not merely legally right but humanly just, so long as one party regards himself only or pre-eminently as an owner of wood, and has only this limited and particular consciousness of himself, while the other is also not regarded as a human being but is seen only as a stealer of wood. From both points of view, it is an inanimate thing, an 'objective force', something inhuman – mere wood – which determines the human being and 'subsumes' him under itself so long as he is incapable of organising and dominating his relations with things in a human and social way. Mere 'wood' can determine man, because, like the commodity, it is an objective expression of essentially political relations; because it has, like the commodity, a fetish-istic character. Therefore, 'the wooden idols can triumph while human beings are sacrificed'.

> If, therefore, wood and the owners of wood make laws, these laws will vary only in respect of the geographical region where, and the language in which, they are promul-gated. This depraved materialism, this sin against the holy ghost of peoples and of humanity, is a direct consequence of that doctrine preached to legislators by the *Preussische Staatszeitung*, urging them to think only of timber and forest in framing the forestry laws, and not to resolve particular material problems politically, i.e. not in relation to the entire reason and morality of the state.
>
> (Marx, 'Debatten über das Holzdiebstahlgesetz')

In so far as something like wood, this apparent 'thing-in-itself', becomes, on the basis of specific social conditions, the determinant of man's being and conduct, human consciousness becomes 'reified' and things themselves become the measure of man. Human relations become reified since material relations become 'humanised' as quasi-personal powers over man. This inversion is a 'depraved materialism'.

This radical-humanist significance of his economic analysis was later critically reinforced by Marx. In *The Holy Family* he asserted against Proudhon that a purely economic interpre-tation of social conditions, such as is involved in the demand for an equal distribution of property, 'in itself still represents an alienated expression' of universal human alienation.

The fact that Proudhon wants to abolish poverty and the

old forms of property is equivalent to wanting to end man's practical alienation from his objective being, the economic expression of human alienation. But because his critique of political economy is still entangled in the presuppositions of political economy, the reappropriation of the objective world is itself still conceived in terms of the economic form of property.

Proudhon contrasts . . . the old form of possession, private property, with ownership. He regards ownership as a 'social function'. This function, however, is not concerned with excluding the other, but with setting in motion and realising man's own potentialities.

Proudhon did not succeed in giving this idea an adequate expression. The conception of 'equal possessions' is itself still an economic, hence still alienated, expression of the idea that the object determines man's being, is his objective being, his being for others, his human relation to other men, and the social relation of man to man. Proudhon overcomes economic alienation (only) within the framework of economic alienation.[15]

That is to say that Proudhon does not, by this means, really overcome alienation at its roots.

The same question as is posed in Marx's article on thefts of wood also appears in *The German Ideology*, although it is formulated in a different way. Here too, Marx asks why men are related in an 'alien' fashion to their own products, so that they no longer control their 'mode of interaction', 'their interrelations become reified against themselves' and 'their own life powers acquire dominance over them'. How is it that within 'the involuntary transformation of personal interest into class interest that personal behaviour of the individual must be reified and alienated, and at the same time emerges as an independent power beyond human control'?[16] Marx finds the answer in the division of labour, which is the basis of rationalisation. The whole preceding style of working must be transcended and transformed into a total 'self-activity'. This transformation means the supersession of the division of labour not only between intellectual and manual work, but also between town and country, which is 'the crassest expression of the subordination of the individual to the division of

labour'.[17] But the division of labour can be genuinely super-
seded only on the basis of a communist social order, which
makes not only property, but human existence in all its manifestations, universal. Within the division of labour, on the
contrary, social relations inevitably acquire an independent
existence as relations between things; this is as inevitable as
the (non-communist) distinction 'between the life of a particular
individual in its personal aspect and his life as it is defined by
some branch of labour and its associated conditions'.[18]

In 1856, ten years after writing *The German Ideology*, Marx
restated his basic view of this inverted world in a retrospective
examination of the revolution of 1848:

There is one great fact, characteristic of this our nineteenth
century, a fact which no party dares deny. On the one hand,
there have started into life industrial and scientific forces
which no epoch of former human history had ever sus-
pected. On the other hand, there exist symptoms of decay,
far surpassing the horrors recorded of the latter times of the
Roman Empire. In our days everything seems pregnant with
its contrary. Machinery, gifted with the wonderful power of
shortening and fructifying human labour, we behold starv-
ing and overworking it. The new-fangled sources of wealth,
by some strange weird spell, are turned into causes of want.
The victories of art seem bought by the loss of character. At
the same pace that mankind masters nature, man seems to
become enslaved to other men or to his own infamy . . .
All our invention and progress seem to result in endowing
material forces with intellectual life, and in stultifying human
life into a material force. This antagonism between modern
industry and science on the one hand, modern misery and
dissolution on the other hand; this antagonism between the
productive powers and the social relations of our epoch is
a fact, palpable, overwhelming, and not to be controverted.
Some parties may wail over it; others may wish to get rid
of modern arts, in order to get rid of modern conflicts. Or
they may imagine that so signal a progress in industry wants
to be completed by as signal a regress in politics. On our
part, we do not mistake the shape of the shrewd spirit that
continues to mark all these contradictions. We know that to
work well the new-fangled forces of society, they only want

to be mastered by new-fangled men – and such are the working men.[19]

The identity of these 'new men' who are called upon to abolish the universal alienation is already clear to Marx in his introduction to the 'Critique of Hegel's Philosophy of Right': 'they are the workers.' With this, the philosophy of 'real humanism' found its appropriate 'social praxis', the means of realising and transcending itself, in the form of 'scientific socialism'. Marx accomplished the decisive break with Feuerbach's 'real humanism' in *The German Ideology*.

Yet even *Capital* is not simply a critique of political economy, but a critique of man in bourgeois society in terms of its economy. The 'economic kernel' of this economy is the commodity form of the product of labour. The commodity (like the 'wood' in the earlier article) is an economic expression of alienation. This alienation consists in the fact that something which was originally intended for use is not directly produced as a useful thing to satisfy one's own need, but enters the modern market as an independent commodity value (regardless of whether it is a material or an intellectual product, whether the market is one for cattle or for books) and only in this roundabout way does it pass from the seller, for whom it has only exchange value, to the consumer as a buyer of commodities.[20] This transformation of the useful object into a commodity exemplifies again the general condition that in bourgeois-capitalist society the product dominates human beings, and not conversely, which would be the 'natural state of affairs' (to use Weber's tentative phrase).

In order to reveal the process whereby this inversion recurred Marx undertook an analysis of the 'reified appearance' of the modern social relations of labour in terms of the 'fetishism' of commodities. As a commodity, an ordinary table is a 'sensuous-suprasensuous' thing.[21] What is immediately apparent to the senses is that which it is as an object for use, and not as a commodity. As a commodity which costs money – because it costs labour or labour time – it is an initially concealed social relationship. In this way, the table 'not only stands with its feet on the ground, but also stands on its head relative to all other commodities, and develops out of its wooden head far more curious whims than if it spontaneously began to dance'.

The secret of the commodity form consists simply in the fact that it mirrors for men the social character of their own labour as an objective characteristic of the labour products themselves, as social natural qualities of these things. Consequently, the social relation of the producers to their aggregate labour presents itself to them as a social relation between objects existing independently of themselves. Through this *quid pro quo* the products of human labour become commodities – sensuous-suprasensuous or social objects . . . It is only the specific social relations among people which here assume for them the phantasmagorical form of a relation among things. To find an analogy, we must enter the nebulous realm of religion. There, the products of the human mind seem to be endowed with a life of their own and appear as independent forms related to each other and to human beings. The same thing happens to the products of the human hand in the world of commodities. I call this the fetishism which adheres to the products of labour as soon as they are produced in the form of commodities and is therefore inseparable from commodity production.[22]

Because the producers of commodities (i.e. the producers of objects of every kind with the form or structure of commodities) enter into human-social relationships only through the exchange of commodities as commodities – hence as 'things' – the social relations which underlie commodities do not appear to the producers themselves as social relations of the human social labour process. On the contrary, these real underlying social relations seem to them to be purely 'objective' relations among themselves as producers, while conversely, the objective relations between commodities assume the character of quasi-personal relations between commodity-entities which act independently in a commodity market which has its own laws.[23]

At first men are not aware of this inversion, for their own self-consciousness is correspondingly reified. But Marx also indicated that he did not regard this inversion only as a social and economic form which has developed in a particular way and no other, but as one which is historically changeable. At first, however, this capacity to change is veiled in reality by the fixed and consummated value form of the commodity in the money form,[24] so that it seems as if one could change only the price of the commodity, but not the commodity character of useful objects. But Marx argued that it is immediately apparent from a comparison with other historical social and economic relations that such a socially determined economic order in which the product of labour as a commodity confronts its producer as an independent entity is totally perverted. For example, however one may judge the 'dark ages' of medieval Europe, with their relations of personal dependency, the social relations between men in their work at least appear[25] there as their own personal relations and are not 'disguised as social relations among things'. Because, in this case, 'relations of personal dependency constitute the existing basis of society, neither work nor product need assume fantastic forms different from its reality. The natural form of labour, its particularity, and not, as in the case of commodity production, its generality, is here its direct social form.'[26]

As an extension of this historical perspective Marx outlined the possibility of a future communist social system in order to contrast the 'transparency' of its social relationship to its own labour products with the opaque perversity and inhumanity of the modern world of commodities. The world of commodities can therefore only be transcended by a fundamental transformation of all the real conditions of human existence. The reabsorption of the commodity character in the character of products as objects of use would require not only de-capitalisation,[27] but also a necessary reabsorption of the fragmented and reified person into a 'natural' person, whose human nature according to Marx consists in the fact that he is intrinsically a *zoon politikon*.[28]

THE POLITICAL EXPRESSION OF HUMAN SELF-ALIENATION IN BOURGEOIS SOCIETY

> The abstraction of the state as such is to be found only in modern times because the abstraction of private life occurs only in modern times.
>
> The real human being of these modern times is the private person of the present-day state constitution.
>
> (Marx, 'Critique of Hegel's Philosophy of Right')

The specifically political expression of human self-alienation is the inner contradiction between the modern state and bourgeois society, that is to say, between man in bourgeois society and the bourgeois state in itself; the fact that man is partly a private individual and partly a public citizen, but is not, in either aspect, a 'complete' human being (which means, for Marx, a being without contradictions). Marx's criticism of economics, as a critique of 'political economy', is already an indirect critique of the social and political conditions of life of humanity engaged in determinate ecomomic activity. And just as his critique of the commodity concerns the commodity-character of all the objects of our world, their fundamental ontological structure, which is a perverted and reified form of human existence, so the critique of bourgeois society and the bourgeois state concerns the nature of man in civil society as such, a determinate form of human existence, namely, private existence, privatised humanity. Marx presents his thematic critique of the basic socio-political conditions of modern life primarily in his 'Critique of Hegel's Philosophy of Right'[29] and in his polemic against Bruno Bauer's essay on the Jewish question. (The related, but unsystematic, comments in *The Holy Family* can be disregarded here.) Both essays formulate systematically the notion of human self-alienation in its socio-political form. The human particularity which is attacked in these writings is not that of man as an owner of money and commodities, but human particularity as such, in contrast and opposition to the public universality of existence. What is distinctive about bourgeois man, what separates and removes him from the universality of public life, is that his human existence is primarily that of a private individual, and in this sense, 'bourgeois'.

The critique of this particularity of human beings in bourgeois society follows closely, even in details, Hegel's critique of bourgeois society.[30] For 'Hegel is not to be blamed for describing the nature of the modern state as it is, but rather because he presents that which is as the essence of the state', and because, in general, he 'mystifies' the empirical, with the result that the content of his arguments becomes the 'crassest materialism'(!) ('Critique of Hegel's Philosophy of Right'). Hegel is a materialist in so far as he regards the factually given as an inherent necessity and posits it philosophically as an absolute. What Hegel actually describes is, according to Marx, nothing but the pervasive conflict between bourgeois society and the state. 'What is profound in Hegel is that he perceives the separation of bourgeois society and political society as a contradiction. What is false is that he rests content with the mere appearance of its resolution' ('Critique of Hegel's Philosophy of Right'). What Hegel had already recognised, and what was given a central significance by Marx, is the fundamentally private character of man in bourgeois society. A particular status in bourgeois society has, therefore, by virtue of its private character, no political character at all.

> The real citizen finds himself in a dual organisation: the bureaucratic, which is an external formal determination of the separated state, the governmental power which does not touch the citizen in his independent reality, and the social, the organisation of civil society. But in the latter sphere, he stands as a private individual outside the state: the private sphere does not touch the political state as such . . . In order to act as a real citizen, to acquire political significance and effectiveness, he must depart from his reality as a citizen, abstract himself from it, and retire from this whole organized life into his individuality; for the only kind of existence available to him as a citizen is his pure, unalloyed individuality, because the existence of the state as a government is assured without him and his existence in civil society is assured without the state. Only in contradiction to these already existing communities, only as an individual can he be a citizen. His existence as a citizen is an existence lying outside his communal existence, and is therefore purely individual.[31]

This division between particular and general interests, which divides the human beings themselves who live in it between a predominantly private but yet public existence, is what Marx combats as human self-alienation. For as a citizen the bourgeois – because he is for himself a private individual – is necessarily something other than himself, external and alien to himself, just as alien as, on the other side, his private life is to the state. His state is an 'abstract' state because, as a bureaucratic, rationalised administrative organisation, it abstracts itself from the real, that is, private, life of its citizens, just as they are, as individuals, abstract themselves from the state. Present-day bourgeois society as a whole, therefore, is the realised principle of individualism; individual existence is its ultimate goal, for which everything else is only a means. The human vocation to be a member of the state necessarily remains an 'abstract' vocation as long as the real conditions of modern life presuppose a separation of real life from political life. As a private individual, in contrast to the public, universal sphere, modern man himself is only a private form of human being. In communist communal life it is just the opposite; there individuals, as individuals, participate fully and personally in the state as their *res publica*.[32]

In a letter of 1843 Marx declared his intention of eliciting 'from the forms of existing reality itself the true reality for which it strives as its ultimate goal', and from the conflict within a state which is fundamentally unpolitical because it is only political, a conflict also within the human being in bourgeois society, in order to discover, through this critique of a world which has grown old, a new world.[33] In fact, the 'positive' elaboration of his conception of a human society and of human beings is developed entirely and solely as a critical transcendence of the – presupposed – contradiction in bourgeois society between public and private life. The privatised humanity of the bourgeois individual is to be transcended in a form of communal life which encompasses the whole being of man, including his 'theoretical' existence, and transforms him into a universal, communist being; in explicit contrast to that 'real' communism (of Cabet, Weitling and others) which is itself still an 'isolated, dogmatic abstraction' because it is still a 'manifestation of the humanistic principle infected by its opposite, by private life'.[34] Indeed, 'the whole socialist principle' conceived in this way is only one side of the full 'reality of authentic human life'.

This radical reduction and destruction of all modes of existence which have become separate and autonomous also corresponds with the reassumption by human beings themselves of all religious particularities. For religion is no longer the 'basis', but only a 'phenomenon', the mode of appearance of human limitations; while the real basis, on the contrary, is the limitation of human life itself to the private individual, a kind of limitation which was unknown either in antiquity or in the Middle Ages.[35]

Marx expounds his rejection of the religious particularity of man in his discussion of Bruno Bauer's writings on the Jewish question. Already in the first sentence, he goes beyond the apparently more practical question of how the Jews might be politically emancipated in Germany. A political emancipation of the Jews would have no significance unless they were also 'humanly' emancipated. But according to Marx neither the Jews nor the Germans (who were to emancipate them) were emancipated in that sense. 'Why should their particular yoke be irksome when they accept the general yoke?' Marx agrees with Bauer that as long as the state is Christian and the Jew is Jewish they are equally incapable, the one of conferring emancipation (i.e. human emancipation) and the other of receiving it. This reduction of the question to one of purely 'human' relationships is considered by both Marx and Bauer to be the only 'critical' and 'scientific' procedure. But at the point where the problem ceases to be theological Bauer ceases to be critical, and here Marx takes his own course by exploring the relation between political emancipation and human emancipation. The limits of merely political emancipation are evident in the fact that 'the state may be a free state without man himself being a free man'. What is needed for a genuine emancipation of the Jews, as of the Christians, is not freedom of religion decreed by the state, but human freedom from religion as such. The problem therefore is a universal and fundamental one, which concerns emancipation from every kind of particularity in human life as a whole; from the specialisation of occupations just as much as from religion and privatisation which separate the individual from general social interests.

> The difference between the religious person and the citizen is the same as that between the shopkeeper and the citizen, between the day-labourer and the citizen, between the landowner and the citizen, between the living individual and the citizen. The contradiction in which the religious man finds himself with the political man is the same contradiction in which the bourgeois finds himself with the *citoyen*, and the member of civil society with his political lion's skin.[36]

But Bauer disregards this rupture between the political state and civil society – these 'worldly' oppositions – and directs his polemic only against their religious expression. This splitting of humanity into Jew and citizen, or Protestant and citizen, is not so much a deception practised against citizenship, but a purely political mode of emancipation from religion. The particularisation of religion is itself merely an expression of the pervasive fragmented condition of modern man in bourgeois society, and simply represents the general 'distancing of man from man', his self-alienation (that is to say, the subjective distinction between 'individual life and species life').

> We do not say to the Jews, therefore, as does Bauer: you cannot be emancipated politically without emancipating yourselves completely from Judaism. We say rather: it is because you can be emancipated politically without renouncing Judaism completely and absolutely that political emancipation itself is not human emancipation. If you Jews want to be politically emancipated, without emancipating yourselves humanly, the inadequacy and the contradiction is not entirely in yourselves but in the nature and the category of political emancipation. If you are imprisoned within this category then you are sharing a general confinement. Just as the state evangelises when, although it is a state, it adopts a Christian attitude towards the Jews, so the Jew politicises when, although a Jew, he demands the rights of citizenship.[37]

Marx goes on to show the incompleteness of emancipation in the limited character of the rights of man in France and America. Here too it is evident that the *droits de l'homme* were not human rights but bourgeois privileges, because this particular, historically situated *homme* as *citoyen* was differentiated from himself as bourgeois. The Declaration of the Rights of Man thus posited – *de facto* – man as bourgeois, the private person as the essential and authentic person.

> None of the so-called rights of man, therefore, go beyond the egoistic man; man as a member of civil society, an individual separated from the community, withdrawn into himself and wholly preoccupied with his private interest and private caprice. Man is far from being considered, in the rights of man, as a species-being; on the contrary, species-life itself, society, appears as a system which is external to the individual, and as a limitation of his original independence. The

only bond between men is natural necessity, need and private interest, the preservation of their property and their egoistic person.[38]

Genuine human emancipation, therefore, has yet to be achieved.

Political emancipation is a reduction of man, on the one hand to a member of civil society, an independent and egoistic individual, and on the other hand to a citizen . . . Human emancipation will only be complete when the real individual person has absorbed into himself the abstract citizen; when as an individual, in his everyday life, in his work, and in his relationships, he had become a species-being; when he has recognised and organised his own powers (*forces propres*) as social powers so that he no longer separates this social power from himself as political power.[39]

The freedom which, in Marx's conception, man is to attain through emancipation is therefore freedom in the sense of Hegel's philosophy of the state; that is, a freedom within the highest degree of community, by contrast with the apparent freedom of the 'isolated individual'. And since the member of the Greek *polis* was freer in this respect than man in bourgeois society, and Christianity is also 'democratic' in terms of its basic principles in so far as it treats every man as a 'sovereign being', Marx is able to say:

Man's self-esteem, his freedom, has first to be reanimated in the human breast. Only this feeling, which vanished from the world with the Greeks, and with the Christians disappeared into the blue haze of the heavens, can create once more out of society a human community, a democratic state, in which men's highest purposes can be attained.[40]

Genuine personal freedom will become possible only in such a community, which responds to the intrinsic nature of human beings, through a social change brought about in human existence and self-consciousness (a change which can come about neither purely internally nor purely externally). By contrast, the private individual of bourgeois society is free only in his own fancy; in reality he is totally dependent and 'subsumed under objective forces'.[41]

THE DIRECT SOCIAL EXPRESSION OF HUMAN SELF-ALIENATION IN THE PROLETARIAT

> If socialist writers ascribe this world-historical role to the proletariat, this is not at all because they regard the proletarians as gods. On the contrary.
>
> (Marx, *The Holy Family*, 'Critical comment no. 2 on Proudhon')

The introduction to the 'Critique of Hegel's Philosophy of Right' already contains this sentence: 'The dissolution of society, as a particular status, is the proletariat.' The positive possibility of human emancipation resides in the proletariat, not because it is a particular class of bourgeois society, but because, and in so far as, it is a society outside society,

> which claims no traditional status but only a human status, which is not opposed to particular consequences but is totally opposed to the assumptions of the German political system; a sphere, finally, which cannot emancipate itself without emancipating itself from all the other spheres of society, without, therefore, emancipating all these other spheres, which is, in short, a total loss of humanity and can only redeem itself by a total redemption of humanity.[42]

With the proletariat, understood in this sense, Marx's philosophy, for which man as a 'species-being' is the highest being, found its natural weapon, while conversely the proletariat found its intellectual weapon in Marx's philosophy. 'Philosophy is the head of this emancipation and the proletariat is its heart.' Similarly, in *The Holy Family* Marx observes that while the propertied class and the proletariat represent fundamentally the same self-alienation, the former class feels itself satisfied and confirmed in this self-alienation and has no critical consciousness of its condition, whereas the other class is one which is 'conscious of its dehumanisation and consequently seeks to overcome it'. The proletariat is, so to speak, the self-consciousness of the 'commodity' because it must alienate itself just like a commodity, but precisely by doing so it develops a critical-revolutionary consciousness, a class-consciousness. In a certain sense, however, the proletarian is less dehumanised than the bourgeois, because he is so in a way which is clearly apparent, not concealed from him or idealised.[43] Because the proletariat concentrates in its conditions of life all the conditions of life of the whole of modern society 'at the peak of their inhumanity' it cannot emancipate itself without thereby emancipating the whole society. This universal-human function of the proletariat is developed further in *The German Ideology* with reference to the universality of the modern world-economy and intercourse.

> Only the present-day proletarians, who are excluded from all autonomous activity, are capable of asserting their complete and unconfined autonomous activity, which consists in the appropriation of a totality of productive forces and the consequent development of a totality of abilities. All previous revolutionary appropriations were limited in scope; individuals whose activity had been restricted by a limited instrument of production and limited intercourse could only appropriate this limited instrument and consequently attain only new forms of limitation. Their instrument of production became their property, but they themselves continued to be subordinated to the division of labour and their own instrument of production. In all previous appropriations a mass of individuals remained subordinate to a single instrument of production, but when the proletarians carry out their appropriation, a mass of production tools must be subordinated to each individual and property must be subordinated to all. Modern universal intercourse can only be subordinated to the individual by being subordinated to all.[44]

Thus, it is not because the proletarians are seen as 'gods', but because the proletariat embodies for Marx the universally human, the species-being in its negation, in the extremity of self-alienation, that it has a fundamental and universal significance, analogous to the commodity character of all modern objects. Because the wage-labourer is completely externalised through the 'mundane problems of life', because he is in no way a 'man', but simply one who valorises and sells his labour power, a personified commodity, his condition has a universal function. In him the economy manifests itself most clearly as human destiny, and with the central significance of the proletariat as the kernel of the modern social problem the economy necessarily becomes the 'anatomy' of bourgeois society. With the self-emancipation of the proletariat, as the universal stratum which has no particular interest to assert, the private mode of human existence is dissolved, along with private property and the private-capitalist economy, which constitute the basic elements of its private character. It is transcended in the universal humanity of a community with communal property and a communal economy in which all its members participate. The mere non-dependence of the bourgeois individual is replaced by the positive freedom of the highest degree of community, which is neither the community of the 'smallest forms of local community' nor the 'direct relationships among individuals',[45] but the community of public life.

Marx did not investigate, in the manner of a specialised empirical sociology, simply the connections, relationships, correspondences and 'interactions'[46] between separate and essentially equivalent spheres of reality, or factors, the sum of which is taken to constitute reality as a whole. He was no abstract empiricist.[47] Just as little, however, was he an abstract philosophical materialist bent upon deducing everything from the economy alone. Rather, Marx analysed the coherent totality of our human world in terms of human self-alienation, which he saw as culminating in the proletariat. Self-alienation, in turn, is regarded from the aspect of its possible transcendence, which for Marx meant no more and no less than transcending the *bourgeois contradictions* (as Hegel had formulated them) of particularity and universality, the private and the public sphere, in a society which would be not only *classless* but *de*-rationalised in *every* respect, and in which 'man as such' is a social species-being.[48] The fact that this self-alienation is 'determined' by the mode and the stage of development of 'material' production, and by the 'natural' division of labour – or in general by the sum of concrete life conditions – does not imply that it is nothing more than the product of a particular, purely economic distortion. It results neither from pure, insubstantial 'inwardness' nor from pure, massive 'externalities', for the two are not separable if 'man' is the 'world' of human beings, his 'life' is the 'expression of life', and his 'self-consciousness' is 'world-consciousness'.

The German Ideology, and to some extent *The Holy Family*, advance beyond the 'Critique of Hegel's Philosophy of Right', not by abandoning the principle of human self-alienation but rather by making it more concrete. The conception becomes more concrete, not by basing it upon an abstract economic factor as cause, but by integrating it with the concretely differentiated context of the factual conditions of life, and giving the category, man, a concrete-historical determination.[49] 'Real' man is also, however, not just man 'in his accidental existence . . . as he comes and goes . . . as he is objectified through the whole organisation of our society', this mere 'appearance' of himself; his 'true reality' lies in the idea of man.

Marx's idea of man is no more speculative than that of any other critic of society, but neither is it something empirically given. The reality upon which it depends, Marx was convinced, is the problem of society in its historical trend of development, and this 'reality provokes the thought' rather than the 'thought trying to capture reality'. Certainly, Marx had 'settled accounts' with his philosophical conscience' in *The German Ideology*, but in contrast with the 'scientific science'[50] of so many Marxists, he still possessed a philosophical conscience, and this conscience not only induced Marx the Hegelian to expound the 'real conditions' of human existence, but also restrained him from making something unconditional out of those conditions, from dissolving 'consciousness' in 'social being' or vice versa. Instead, Marx wanted to realise philosophy by transcending it and to transcend it through this realisation.[51] The form and manner of his proposed realisation of philosophy is, however, necessarily determined by what he encountered as the 'truly existing' within what exists, and what, accordingly, in the last analysis, he desired – which was something very different from Weber.

NOTES

1 Korsch, 1923, p. 74, n. 66. Nevertheless, in *Theories of Surplus Value*, Vol. I, we read: 'Man himself is the basis of his material production, as of all production which he accomplishes. All circumstances, therefore, which affect man, the subject of production, have a greater or lesser influence upon all his functions and activities, including his functions and activities as the creator of material wealth, of commodities.'

2 Karl Marx, Friedrich Engels, *MEGA*, I/1/1. This refers to the first half-volume, in the first volume of the first section of *Karl Marx/ Friedrich Engels: Historisch-Kritische Gesamtausgabe*, ed. D. Riazanov (1927 onwards) [Eds].

3 See Seillière, 1911.

4 See Löwith, 'Hegel und Hegelianismus', in *Zeitschrift für deutsche Bildung*, November 1931.

5 The fact that 'cosmopolitanism' can enter into opposition to the life of the state shows that Hegel understood by this term a kind of internationalism. See note 38 for the contrary view of cosmopolitanism expressed by Marx.

6 This fundamental difference in the definition of the human being (through Hegel and Feuerbach to Marx) which characterises the development of philosophy in the nineteenth century, is brought within a unitary conception to some extent in Heidegger's ontological definition of man as an 'existent' (*Dasein*). See my review and criticism in *Theoligische Rundschau*, nos 1 and 5, and in *Zeitschrift für Theologie und Kirche*, no. 5.

7 See Löwith, 'Feuerbach und der Ausgang der klassischen deutschen Philosophie', *Logos*, 1928, and Löwith, 1928, pp. 5–13; cf. also Ruge's similar critique of para. 190 of Hegel's *Philosophy of Right* in *Aus früherer Zeit*, Vol. IV, p. 359.

8 'My first endeavour was to make philosophy the concern of humanity. But whoever embarks on this path necessarily comes to make man the concern of philosophy and to transcend philosophy itself; for it becomes a human concern only when it ceases to be philosophy (that is, segregated academic philosophy)' (Feuerbach, op. cit.). Marx reiterated this principle in a more discriminating form when he claimed that 'making the world philosophical' (as with Hegel) would necessarily 'make philosophy worldly', so that its 'realisation' would also be its 'loss'. Herder already posed the question: 'How can philosophy be reconciled with human affairs and politics so that it really serves them?'; and he answered by calling for a 'withdrawal' of philosophy into 'anthropology'.

9 Marx, *The Holy Family*.

10 The difference between Marx and Feuerbach, which is most concisely summarised in the well-known 'Theses on Feuerbach', may be characterised in general terms as follows: Marx, basing himself upon Feuerbach's anthropological approach, counterposed the content of Hegel's doctrine of objective spirit to Feuerbach's abstract I–thou formulation of the problem. He turns against Feuerbach because the latter has made merely 'abstract' man, that is, man divorced from the 'world', the basis of philosophy. It is just this 'world' of political and economic conditions of life, however, which Hegel's *Philosophy of Right* made apparent. What remains uncontested is only Feuerbach's achievement in going back from Absolute Spirit to the natural man. But the way in which he defined the human being – namely, exclusively as a naturalistic species-being, and in terms of his sensuous existence and relation to the other – demonstrated to Marx that Feuerbach had only 'set aside' Hegel and had not critically transcended him. Feuerbach had constructed a human being who at best reflected in his reality the bourgeois private individual. His theory of 'I and thou', like the bourgeois private individual in practice, leads back to private

relationships between individuals in assumed 'love' and 'friend-ship', without recognising that not only the apparent 'purely human' conditions of life, but also the most simple objects of 'sense perception', are shaped and given to him by the general social and economic conditions of his world (*The German Ideology*). So Marx is in the position of using Hegel's concrete analyses in the *Philosophy of Right* – which he is demolishing from the point of view of their philosophical claims – against Feuerbach and on the other hand attacking Hegel from Feuerbach's anthropological standpoint. He defends Hegel against Feuerbach because Hegel has expressed the decisive significance of the general and social course of events for each individual, and he attacks Hegel because he has philo-sophically absolutised and mystified these general conditions. But Feuerbach himself was aware of the preliminary character of his theses, as is clearly shown by the preface to his *Principles*, which ends by saying that the 'consequences' of his principles of the philosophy of the 'future' would not fail to appear. These con-clusions (consequences) were drawn by Marx.

11 Marx was convinced from the outset that man is by nature 'man in society', that is, a social being; it is the *conditio sine qua non* of his anthropology. 'If man is social by nature, he only develops his true nature in society, and the power of his nature should be measured not by the power of the single individuals but by the power of society' (*The Holy Family*; cf. the preface to *Contribution to the Critique of Political Economy*, and the tenth thesis on Feuerbach).

12 Lukács, 1923, section 1 of 'Reification and the consciousness of the proletariat', which demonstrated for the first time the fundamental structure and meaning of Marx's analysis of the commodity from a Hegelian perspective.

13 Marx's article, 'Debatten über das Holzdiebstahlgesetz' was pub-lished in the *Rheinische Zeitung*, October–November 1842, and reprinted in *MEGA* I/1/1 [Eds].

14 *Differenz der demokritischen und epikureischen Naturphilosophie* (Doc-toral dissertation, 1841, published in *MEGA* I/1/1 [Eds]).

15 *The Holy Family*. See the analogous account, in the 'Critique of Hegel's Philosophy of Right', of the impossibility of overcoming human self-alienation within a state which is still 'political', whether its form is monarchical or republican.

16 *The German Iedology*, pt III, 'Saint Max'.

17 *The German Ideology*, pt I, section B, 'The real basis of ideology'. The particular attention which Weber, in *Economy and Society*, devoted to the historical sociology of the city again shows clearly the factual identity of self-alienation and rationalisation.

18 See *The German Ideology*, and also Engels, *Anti-Dühring*. Engels's irony about Dühring's 'hucksters and architects' is analogous to Marx's observation that 'Originally there is less difference between a porter and a philosopher than between a watch dog and a borzoi. It is the division of labour which has produced a chasm between them.'

19 Address at the Fourth Anniversary Banquet of the *People's Paper*. Published in *People's Paper*, 19 April 1856.

20 In this dual character of the commodity there is expressed a specific inner division in the commodity-producing society itself; for the commodity itself is a 'social substance' – abstract human-social labour. In his account of the stock exchange Weber still presented this separation of production and consumption in purely Marxian terms.

21 This analysis of Marx shows indirectly the social limits of Heidegger's analysis, in *Sein und Zeit*, of the 'world of products' (*Werkwelt*). Through the orientation of all inner-worldly being to the existence (*Da-sein*) of each individual, not only is the problem of the social nature of existence reduced to that of the 'one' (*man*), but at the same time the social character of our objects of use – of the available 'product' – remains unexplored in its ontological distinctiveness. The fact that our product has the character of a commodity and that the commodity is a 'social' substance only becomes apparent when existence itself is conceived not only as an essential and public community with others, but also as one in which each individual, and all individuals together, acquire a universal character through society. The manner in which they are 'universalised' in bourgeois society is such that society becomes a society of 'particularised individuals', an 'abstract universality' and thereby obscures its own social character. (See Marx's preface to *Contribution to the Critique of Political Economy*.) But in order to characterise Heidegger's existentialist philosophy as 'petty-bourgeois', as has been done by both Marxists and non-Marxists, one would have to be bold enough to assert that its principle of individuation – death – is a petty-bourgeois phenomenon. Tolstoy inferred from the fact of death the senselessness of the whole social process of civilisation. (See Weber, 'Science as a vocation'.)

22 *Capital*, Vol. I, ch. 1, section 4.

23 In fact this 'following of its own laws' is not an *immediate* fact from which one could begin (and have to relativise it later) but a mediated result of the acquisition of autonomy. See Engels's letter to C. Schmidt, 27 October 1890.

24 See *Capital*, Vol. III, ch. 21, on the fetishistic character of interest-bearing capital.

25 In *Capital* Marx regards it as self-evident that this is mere appearance, a 'character mask', behind which in every instance the domination of the conditions of production over the producers is concealed (see *Capital*, Vol. III, ch. 48).

26 *Capital*, Vol. I, ch. 1, section 4.

27 On the connection between the two, see especially the methodical summary in *Capital*, Vol. I, ch. 4, and Marx's letter to Engels of 22 June 1867.

28 From a historical point of view, it is highly significant that what Marx rejected as the 'alienation' of modern humanity, and Weber accepted as 'inexorable fate', Hegel could still justify in a positive

manner. In the *Philosophy of Right* (para. 67) Hegel argued that man may externalise specific products and a temporally limited use of his particular bodily and mental capacities for activity, because they have, within this limitation, only an 'external' relationship to human 'totality' and 'universality'. This personal externalisation Hegel explicitly equated with man's relation to things. With regard to this relation he argued (para. 61) that a thing attains its true end precisely and only when it is used by man for the purpose for which it exists (in accordance with its nature). Only the full utilisation of the thing – even though this is apparently quite 'external' to the thing 'in itself' – establishes its full validity in terms of what it is. Hence, the 'externality' of the thing, realised through its utilisation, is its essential substance. Using a thing is therefore equivalent to having it for oneself (*eigen*), and this is the original sense of 'ownership' (*Eigentum*). Likewise, the totality of human life expression and the total utilisation of human powers is identical with the totality of the substance of life itself.

From this identity of the substance of personal life with the totality of its expression, however, there does not follow at all the conclusion which Hegel drew; namely, that a particular specific productive activity within a limited daily period of time could not for all that, destroy the genuine totality of the whole human being, and make him a particularised, alienated being, whatever the philosophical 'externality' of such an activity. But Hegel's philosophy, which posited 'spirit' as the 'universal' of humanity, was not concerned with this unreasonable reality. Hence there appears the following extraordinary addendum (to para. 67): 'The difference analysed here is the difference between a slave and a present-day domestic servant or day-labourer. The Athenian slave had perhaps lighter tasks and more intelligent work than our servants generally have, but he was still a slave because the whole range of his activity was externalised.'

Marx drew precisely the opposite conclusion; namely, that the legally 'free' wage-labourer is in reality less free than the slave of antiquity, since although he is legally the free owner of his labour and the equal of the owner of the means of production, and although he does not sell himself but 'only' his labour power, for a limited period of time, he becomes thereby wholly a commodity, for his saleable labour power is all that he really 'owns', and he *must* externalise it in order to live (*Capital*, Vol. I, ch. 4, section 3). This 'free' wage-slave, however, also embodies for Marx the universal problem of modern commodity-producing society, whereas the slave of antiquity stood altogether outside 'human' society, which was all that was considered, so that his fate had no general significance. (Compare the 'candidly' cynical form of the Hegelian distinction between human totality and externality in Hugo's *Natural Right*, para. 144, and Marx's critique in 'The philosophical manifesto of the historical school of laws', *Rheinische Zeitung*, 9 August 1842.)

29 On this, and on the question of dating, which is not unimportant for the interpretation, see E. Lewalter, 'Zur Systematik der Marxschen Staats- und Gesellschaftslehre', *Archiv für Sozialwissenschaft und Sozialpolitik*, Vol. LXVI, 1932.

30 See A. Ruge, 'Die Hegelsche Rechtsphilosophie und die Politik unserer Zeit', *Deutsch Jahrbücher für Wissenschaft und Kunst*, 1842.

31 'Critique of Hegel's Philosophy of Right'. The pertinence of this characterisation is shown not least by the opposed conclusion which Max Weber drew from it.

32 *The German Ideology*, pt 1, section C, 'Communism'. At the same time Marx pointed out that the difference between the 'personal' and the relatively 'accidental' individual has quite a different meaning in different periods and different societies; thus, for example, his 'status' or family membership may have an accidental meaning for the eighteenth-century individual, but a highly personal significance at other times. In each case, therefore, it is a particular sphere of life which determines the distinctive character of the true and general concept of 'man' and 'individual'. This sphere, for man in the bourgeois era, is the private sphere.

33 See Marx's letter of September 1843 to Ruge (subsequently published in the *Deutsch-Französische Jahrbücher*, 1844 [Eds]). Ten years later, in 1852, Marx presented a concise historical account of this 'world grown old' in *The Eighteenth Brumaire of Louis Bonaparte*. He interprets this stage of the bourgeois revolution as a self-caricature of the great bourgeois revolution of 1789. The passions of this epoch are without truth, and its truths without passion; its reality, which has become entirely 'sober and insipid', can only be borne through borrowings, its development is a constant repetition of the same tensions and relaxations, its contradictions of a kind which rise to a peak only to be blunted and then collapse, its history a history without events, its heroes without heroic deeds, and its first law indecision. Seen in terms of the history of the period it is unmistakable how much Kierkegaard, with his 'Critique of the present time', is a contemporary of Marx, and how both of them embody in their work a decisive break with Hegel's philosophy of spirit, though in opposite directions.

34 See for an opposed view, *The German Ideology*, pt 1, section C, 'Communism', where communism is conceived precisely as that which 'really' exists, although its 'reality' is generally described as a 'movement'.

35 The true private person of antiquity was the slave, because he had no part in the *res publica*, but for this very reason he was not a 'human being' in the full sense. Similarly, in the Middle Ages each privage sphere of life also amplified a public sphere. 'The life of the people and the life of the state are identical in the Middle Ages. Man is the true principle of the state, but unfree man.' It was the French revolution which first emancipated man politically as a bourgeois, and thereby developed the private condition as

such into the specific condition of human existence, even though it had intended to make every human being a citizen.

36 Marx, 'On the Jewish question'. See also Ruge's letter to Marx of 1843 where he cites as a 'motto for his orientation' Hölderlin's famous declaration from *Hyperion*: 'You see artisans but no men, thinkers but no men, masters and servants but no men . . .', and Marx's expression of agreement in his reply.

37 'On the Jewish question'.

38 ibid.

39 ibid.

40 Letter to Ruge, May 1843, published in *Deutsch-Frazösische Jahrbücher*. True democracy, therefore, originally meant for Marx 'classless society' in the sense of 'a *polis* perfected into a cosmopolis, a "community of the free" in Aristotle's sense'; cf. Lewalter, op. cit.

41 *The German Ideology*, pt III, section 1, 'The ego and his own.'

42 'Critique of Hegel's Philosophy of Right'.

43 See Lukács's analysis in *History and Class Consciousness*, pp. 173–81.

44 *The German Ideology*, pt 1, section B.3.

45 For Weber this is a consequence of the fact that 'ultimate' values have withdrawn from the 'public realm'. See his essays on 'Science as a vocation' and 'Politics as a vocation', in Gerth and Mills, 1947.

46 See Korsch, op. cit., p. 70, n. 56.

47 *The German Ideology*, pt 1, section A. (Marx derives the term from Hegel.) [It should be noted, however, that Löwith disregards Marx's much more frequent favourable references to empiricism in the same text. Eds.]

48 Species-being (*Gattungswesen*), not in the naturalistic-moralistic sense of Feuerbach, but in the Hegelian sense of a unity of general and private particular interests (see especially *The German Ideology*, pt III, 'Saint Max'). It is self-evident that Marx's de-rationalisation was not conceived as a utopian return to some 'primordial communism', but as a higher stage of rationality in the form of a truly 'rational' regulation of the relations of production as a whole under 'communal control', on the basis of the stage of development of the production process which had been reached. Hence in *Capital*, too, the idea of 'freedom' is reduced to the sober statement that even after this socialisation the 'realm of freedom' begins only 'outside the sphere of material production proper', while within the realm of labour determined by external need and necessity freedom can only consist in the fact that 'socialised humanity, the associated producers, regulate their interchange with nature rationally' (*Capital*, Vol. III, ch. 48, Löwith's italics. [Eds]).

49 *The German Ideology*, especially pt III, 'Saint Max'. See also later, in *The Poverty of Philosophy*, the criticism of the mere 'category' of division of labour.

50 This analogy with Marx's critique of 'critical criticism' comes from Karl Korsch.

51 'Critique of Hegel's Philosophy of Right'.

Chapter 4

Weber's critique of the materialist conception of history

The title under which Weber gave his lectures of 1918 on the sociology of religion was: 'Positive critique of the materialist conception of history'.[1] Ten years earlier, in his criticism of Stammler's 'so-called' surpassing of the materialist interpretation of history,[2] he had already outlined an indirect criticism of Marxism in respect of its basic methodology. The 'materialist conception of history' presupposed by Weber's criticism is not to be found in Marx himself either in substance or under his name, and especially not in the young Marx, who had not yet settled accounts with his 'philosophical conscience'.[3] It is a product of the vulgar economistic 'Marxism' derived from Engels and the later Marx. The original, full content of Marx's critical analysis of man in bourgeois economic society was thereby more or less lost to sight. Weber's misplaced criticism of Marx, which was conditioned by this fact, has affinities with the misunderstanding of the original and comprehensive object of Weber's own sociology in later bourgeois sociology. Just as the latter, with its substantive additions and methodological discussions, obscured Weber's pre-eminent concern with investigating the historical phenomenon of rationalism, so Weber himself – in accord here with the vulgar Marxists – obscured, in his arguments against Marxism, Marx's original and overriding concern with the historical phenomenon of human self-alienation. Yet even in this erroneous form Weber's critique makes evident the real nature of his difference from Marx, which has to be recovered from the mistaken form of his attack upon Marxism, in order to re-establish the difference between Weber and Marx on its original ground.

WEBER'S INDIRECT CRITIQUE OF MARX IN THE DISPUTE WITH STAMMLER

If we disregard the fact that the parody of a dialogue between the assumed social-philosophical 'spiritualists' or even 'materialists' and the sociological 'empiricists' with their 'common sense' (Weber) is only intended to apply directly to Stammler's adoption and modification of the materialist conception of history, and concentrate our attention upon the way in which Weber's attitude towards Stammler expresses a similar attitude towards Marx, then we can derive from the second section of this critique the following scientific exposition by Weber of his own position, and the corresponding view adopted in his criticism of Marx. The spiritualist thesis that 'in the last analysis' human history, including political and economic events, only reflects religious conflicts and is therefore to be explained in a unitary and unambiguous way (and not to be constructed out of numerous intersecting causal chains) is, according to Weber, 'empirically' just as unprovable and incontrovertible as the materialist thesis (opposed only in its content, not in its method) which asserts that 'in the last analysis' economic struggles are the decisive factor in human history.

Weber, the sociological 'empiricist', affirmed against both these positions that no scientific statement at all can be made about the general causal significance of the religious factor for social life in general.[4] Such a dogmatic formulation of the problem has, at best, a 'heuristic' value, but the extent to which it is 'factually' justified can only be determined by historical investigation of particular historical cases. Beyond this, however, it may be possible to arrive at general rules of the historical process. (The real positive outcome of Weber's critique of Stammler is therefore an analysis of the various meanings of possible uniformities.) The scientific total perspective, so far as this is possible, does not consist in the dogmatic extension of a single element, a single factor, into the totality of a 'world formula', of which only 'dogmatists' are convinced, but in an advance from the necessary one-sidedness of every mode of scientific observation which is dictated by specific points of view which limit the features of the object observed, to a many-sided mode of observation. Otherwise, there seems to be no reason why one should not try to derive social life, in the last analysis, 'from the cephalic index, the influence of sunspots, or even from the digestive troubles'.

WEBER'S CRITIQUE OF MARX IN THE SOCIOLOGY OF RELIGION

This very abbreviated account of Weber's critique of Stammler nevertheless shows its close similarity to that expressed in the scattered references to Marx in Weber's sociology of religion.[5] This too is not intended to be a positive critique of the materialist conception of history, in the sense that it opposes to it a spiritualist approach; rather, it aspires to be positive by rejecting, in a fundamental way, every kind of definitive deduction, and putting in its place a 'concrete' historical analysis of the mutual determination of all the factors of historical reality, thus cutting the ground from under any one-sided formulation of either a spiritualist or materialist metaphysics of history. Accordingly, the so-called spirit of capitalism is understood by Weber neither in the vulgar Marxist sense as a merely ideological spirit of capitalist relations of production, nor as an autonomous and primordial religious spirit which is quite independent of capitalism; instead, the spirit of capitalism exists for him only in so far as there is a general tendency towards a rational conduct of life, borne along by the bourgeois stratum of society, which establishes an elective affinity between the capitalist economy on one side and the Protestant ethic on the other.

We should not be misled by the fact that Weber himself, emphasising the critical side of his statements on economic materialism, occasionally gave his basic conception an anti-Marxist character, and referred to this spirit as if it were an 'ethical infrastructure'.[6] He immediately retracted the misleading sharpening of his view: 'no such simplistic doctrinaire thesis should be maintained' as that the 'capitalist spirit . . . could only have arisen from specific influences of the Reformation, or indeed that capitalism as an economic system is a product of the Reformation'. Towards the end of his study Weber stated even more clearly that he had not intended 'to replace a one-sided "materialist" with an equally one-sided "spiritualist" causal account of culture and history. Both are equally possible'; which, properly understood, means that both are, 'scientifically' speaking, equally impossible!⁷ They are not scientifically impossible on the basis of any objective norms of science, but on the basis of a recognition of the destiny of rationalisation as a whole, something of which 'empirical', factual, specialised science is itself an outstanding instance.⁸

In spite of his rejection, based upon these grounds, of a metaphysic of history, Weber's own research into the spirit of capitalism – contrary to his self-image as a specialised scientist – is something quite other than a purely empirical depiction of particular facts, and is therefore a 'course across a boundless ocean'. It is a purely scientific depiction of facts only in the sense that Weber as a person was a 'specialist'. If he was not so 'simplistic and doctrinaire' as to want to deduce the spirit of capitalism purely from a sociology of religion, neither was he so boundlessly active and rudderless as to be content with an agglomeration of abstract empirical data. The 'positive' aspect of his studies, comprehended as a critique of Marx, does not consist indeed in a dogmatic reversal of the vulgar Marxist method, but in a quite different, but fundamental, method of his own. The different character of his method cannot simply be grasped from what he himself says about it, but becomes apparent in its connection with his whole attitude to reality, including that of science.

He himself characterises the difference between his own method and that of Marxism as the difference between an 'empirical' and a 'dogmatic' method. But the real meaning of his 'empirical' procedure lies only apparently in the advance from the necessary 'one-sidedness' of scientific observation to a scientific 'many-sidedness', by contrast with the dogmatic unequivocalness of a world-formula. Its true meaning lies rather in the fact that Weber, by his renunciation of the idea of a 'universal humanity' and all-embracing 'world-formulae', wanted to weaken all commitments to any specific 'givens' whatsoever, and hence also their possible elaboration into an illusory totality. What he contests in practice is not the totality of existence and observation, but the possible rigidification of a particular into a universal; that is, into a specific type of (illusory) totality. The really possible totalisation, which he himself practised, was not the summation of all conceivable particulars into a so-called many-sidedness, but rather the negative one of 'freedom of movement' in all directions, breaking out of every 'cage', every practical and theoretical orientation, order and legitimation, in order to preserve even in science that remnant of 'individualism' which to him signified the truly human.

Even the immense casuistry of his conceptual definitions in *Economy and Society* has a dual purpose; not only to capture and fix reality in definitions, but at the same time and above all to establish the opposite sense of an open system of 'possibilities'.[9] He referred constantly to 'the advantages of the division of labour', and of rationalisation generally, as long as they are 'successful', but at the same time he emphasised the 'unreality' of this one-sidedness of theory in dividing up reality. Yet despite, or rather because of this, he could claim that this kind of sociology is 'a science of reality'. It was truly a science of reality, however, not because it grasped the true reality purely and scientifically in the only possible way, as something unchanging and enduring, but rather because Weber (aware of the uncertainties of our present-day ideals and realities) approached this reality of ours with a freedom of aim alongside the constraints of a rigorous, and hence 'technical', method.[10] The uniqueness of his 'empirical' method thus arises from the fact that he was not bound by any specialised domain of life or science, and combated all 'dogmatic' methods as the scientific form of being trapped in a transcendental attitude of man towards the world, a premature commitment to ostensible 'final' authorities of a religious, social, or even scientific kind.

In fact, Weber did not thereby renounce (as his writings against Stammler might appear to suggest) any kind of mastery and conceptual grasp of the 'whole' in its 'unity', of the possibility of a systematic method. It is merely that the unique and consistent 'principle' underlying his theoretical and practical procedure is far less obvious than the dogmatic-revolutionary principle of Marx. It consists in the recognition of a contradiction: the rational, specialised division of labour and fragmentation of the soul, but in such a way that this rationality is at the same time the problematic locus of freedom. He did not attempt to resolve this contradiction on its own ground, but to master it. Hence, not only Marx but also Weber cannot be refuted on the basis of so-called 'facts', but only in that 'struggle of the gods', of fundamental and consistent standpoints, even though the struggle is carried on with the means of science. It is not only possible, but obligatory, to engage in controversy about 'normative standards' themselves, and 'the struggle does not take place only, as we like to believe nowadays, between "class interests", but also between worldviews; although, of course, it remains perfectly true that the world-view which an individual adopts is decided among many other things, and certainly to a pre-eminent degree, by it elective affinity with his "class interest" (if, for the moment, we accept this concept which is only apparently unambiguous)'.[11]

Accordingly, in his treatment of the 'objectivity' of knowledge in the social sciences Weber was concerned first of all to raise the question 'what is the meaning and purpose of a scientific critique of ideals and value judgements?' And he carried out this inquiry too, in a 'rational' manner, with reference to a responsible relation between means and ends. Such a struggle cannot be avoided, not even through 'relationism',[12] for if what is involved is really a struggle between ultimate principles and the orientations based upon them, then it is not a struggle between particular 'one-sided' aspects and perspectives; each principle has in itself a univeral significance, as the alpha and omega of a basic conception of what is truly real and therefore really worth knowing.

Because Marx and Weber believed they knew what is truly real and truly human in respect of the reality which encompasses us, their science had to do with a 'totality'. This is not the sum of all that exists, but the summation of everything meaningful in the totality of a principle, on the basis of which the whole can be investigated in detail. The totality whose significance both of them recognised from the outset and made the object of their investigations is the problem of the modern world, which is 'capitalist' in its economic aspect and 'bourgeois' in its political aspect. This was already the theme of Weber's inaugural lecture of 1895, 'The National State and Economic Policy', in which he presented some unpalatable truths to his own class in discussing the political failure of both the Prussian Junker class and the bourgeoisie, as well as that of the social-democratic working class. He expressed doubt that the bourgeoisie would be able to raise 'the veil of its illusions', and recognise that Bismarck's legacy had become the curse of its political epigones. The same kind of doubt is echoed in his lecture of 1918 on radical socialism, in which he questions the

Marxist expectation that the abolition of private enterprise would end the domination of man by man.

NOTES

1 See Marianne Weber, 1926, p. 604.
2 Weber, 1907.
3 Preface to *Contribution to the Critique of Political Economy*.
4 Weber assumes that the problem of the 'totality' can only be posed in a 'causal' scientific sense, but this only makes sense if the totality is conceived as a sum of two parts: religion and society. In fact, Weber's own investigation concerns a totality for which the idea of such a summation is untenable; namely, the totality of the historical trend towards rationalisation – a totality which cannot be derived and imputed in specific areas; cf. Lukács's distinction between the 'reality' of general historical trends of development and particular empirical 'facts' (op. cit., pp. 202–3).
5 In Weber, 1904a, esp. pp. 90–2, 183, 277–8, and in the introduction to his essays on 'The economic ethic of the world religions', in Gerth and Mills, 1947, esp. pp. 267–8. See also ' "Objectivity" in social science and social policy', in Shils and Finch, 1949, pp. 68–70.
6 See Kraus, 1930, pp. 234 ff. and pp. 243 ff. The inaccuracy of Kraus's criticism is apparent from Weber's statement referred to in the following note.
7 See Gerth and Mills, 1947, pp. 267–8, 280; and Weber, 1904a, nn. 84, 108, 118–19, on pp. 177–8, 282–4.
8 See Lukács, 1923, pp. 103–5, 183–5.
9 See ' "Objectivity" in social science and social policy', in Shils and Finch, 1949, pp. 84, 102–4; cf. A. Walther, *Jahrbuch für Soziologie*, 1926, pp. 54 ff.
10 See Weber, 1903–6, and *Gesammelte Aufsätze sur Wissenschaftslehre* (Tübingen: Mohr, 1922), pp. 344, 348, 375.
11 ' "Objectivity" in social science and social policy', in Shils and Finch, 1949, p. 56.
12 The reference is to Karl Mannheim's doctrine about the way in which diverse value orientations or world-views might be transcended [Eds].

Bibliography

Burckhardt, Jacob (1955), *The Letters of Jacob Burckhardt* (London: Routledge & Kegan Paul).

Dilthey, Wilhelm (1959, 1962), *Einleitung in die Geisteswissenschaften. Gesammelte Schriften*, Vol. 1 (Stuttgart: Teubner). There are various English translations of excerpts from Dilthey's works.

Engels, Friedrich. See Marx and Engels.

Feuerback, Ludwig (1843), *Grundsätze der Philosophie der Zukunft* (Zurich: Verlag des literarischen Comptoirs).

Freyer, Hans (1930), *Soziologie als Wirklichkeitswissenschaft* (Leipzig and Berlin: Teubner).

Gerth, H. H. and Mills, C. W. (eds) (1947), *From Max Weber* (London: Routledge & Kegan Paul).

Grab, H. J. (1927), *Der Begriff des Rationalen in der Soziologie Max Webers* (Leipzig: Hans Buske Verlag).

Habermas, J. (1972), *Knowledge and Human Interests* (London: Heinemann).

Hegel, G. W. F. (1821), *Philosophy of Right* (Oxford: Clarendon Press, 1942).

Heidegger, Martin (1927), *Being and Time* (London: SCM Press, 1962).

Hess, Moses (1959), *Briefwechsel*, ed. E. Silberner (The Hague: Mouton).

Honigsheim, Paul (1968), *On Max Weber* (New York and London: Collier Macmillan).

Jaspers, Karl (1921), *Rede bei der von der Heidelberger Studentenschaft am 17 Juli 1920 veranstalteten Trauerfeier* (Tübingen: Mohr); repr. in Karl Jaspers, *Rechenschaft und Ausblick* (Munich: Piper, 1951).

Korsch, Karl (1923), *Marxism and Philosophy* (London: New Left Books, 1970).

Kraus, J. B. (1930), *Scholastik, Puritanismus und Kapitalismus* (Munich and Leipzig: Duncker & Humblot).

Landshut, Siegfried (1929), *Kritik der Soziologie* (Munich and Hamburg: Duncker & Humblot; new edn Neuwied and Berlin: Luchterhand, 1969).

Lask, Emil (1902), *Fichtes Idealismus und die Geschichrte* (Tübingen and Leipzig: Mohr).

Löwith, Karl (1928), *Das Individuum in der Rolle des Mitmenschen* (Tübingen: Mohr).

Löwith, Karl (1941), *From Hegel to Nietzsche: The Revolution in Nineteenth-Century Thought* (New York: Holt, Rinehart & Winston, 1964).

Löwith, Karl (1960), *Gesammelte Abhandlungen. Zur Kritik der geschichtlichen Existenz* (Stuttgart: Kohlhammer).

Lukács, Georg (1923), *History and Class Consciousness* (London: Merlin Press, 1971).

Luppol, J. (1929), *Lenin und die Philosophie* (Veinna: Velag für Literatur und Politik).

Mannheim, Karl (1929), *Ideology and Utopia* (London: Routledge & Kegan Paul, 1936).

Marx, Karl and Engels, Friedrich. Since there are numerous editions and translations of the works of Marx and Engels we have given a reference in the notes to the chapter or section of the work being cited, so that the reader can trace the quotation in any available edition.

Mitzman, Arthur (1970), *The Iron Cage: An Historical Interpretation of Max Weber* (New York: Knopf).

Mommsen, Wolfgang (1959), *Max Weber und die deutsche Politik 1890–1920* (Tübingen: Mohr).

Mommsen, Wolfgang (1974), *The Age of Bureaucracy: Perspectives on the Political Sociology of Max Weber* (Oxford: Blackwell).

Musil, Robert (1930–2), *The Man without Qualities*, 3 vols (London: Secker & Warburg, 1953–60).

Nietzsche, Friedrich (1878), *Human, All Too Human* (Edinburgh and London: J. N. Foulis, 1909).

Nietzsche, Friedrich (1886), *Beyond Good and Evil* (Harmondsworth: Penguin, 1973).

Nietzsche, Friedrich (1887), *The Genealogy of Morals* (Garden City, NY: Doubleday, 1956).

Nietzsche, Friedrich (1901), *The Will to Power* (London: Weidenfeld & Nicolson, 1968).

Petrović, Gajo (1967), *Marx in the Mid-Twentieth Century* (Garden City, NY: Doubleday).

Plamenatz, John (1975), *Karl Marx's Philosophy of Man* (Oxford: Clarendon).

Rathenau, Walther (1913), *Zur Mechanik des Geistes* (Berlin: S. Fischer).

Ruge, Arnold (1862), *Aus früherer Zeit*, 4 vols (Berling: Duncker & Humblot).

von Schelting, Alexander (1934), *Max Webers Wissenschaftslehre* (Tübingen: Mohr).

Seillière, Ernest (1911), *Der demokratische Imperialismus: Rousseau – Proudhon – Marx;* originally published as *L'impérialisme démocratique*, Pt III of *La philosophie de l'impérialisme* (Paris: Plon-Nourrit, 1907).

Simmel, Georg (1968), *The Conflict in Modern Culture and Other Essays* (New York: Teachers College Press).

Spann, Othmar (1914), *Kurzgefasstes System der Gesellschaftslehre* (Leipzig: Quelle & Meyer).

Wach, Joachim (1931), *Einführung in die Religionssoziologie* (Tübingen: Mohr).

Weber, Marianne (1926), *Max Weber: A Biography* (New York and London: Wiley Interscience, 1975).

Weber, Max (1903–6), *Roscher and Knies: The Logical Problems of Historical Economics* (New York: Free Press, 1975).

Weber, Max (1904a), *The Protestant Ethic and the Spirit of Capitalism* (London: Allen & Unwin, 1976).

Weber, Max (1904b), ' "Objectivity" in social science and social policy', in E. Shils and H. Finch (eds), *The Methodology of the Social Sciences* (Glencoe, Ill.: Free Press, 1949).

Weber, Max (1907), *Critique of Stammler* (New York: Free Press, 1977).

Weber, Max (1917–19), *Ancient Judaism* (Chicago: Free Press, 1962).

Weber, Max (1919), 'Politics as a vocation', in Gerth and Mills, 1947.

Weber, Max (1920), *Gesammelte Aufsätze zur Religionssoziologie* (Tübingen: Mohr).

Weber, Max (1921a), *Gesammelte Politische Schriften* (Tübingen: Mohr).

Weber, Max (1921b), *Economy and Society*, 3 vols (New York: Bedminster Press, 1968).

Weber, Max (1921c), *The Rational and Social Foundations of Music* (Carbondale, Ill.: Southern Illinois University Press, 1958).

Weber, Max (1922), 'Science as a vocation', in Gerth and Mills, 1947.

Weber, Max (1924a), *Gesammelte Aufsätze zur Soziologie und Sozialpolitik* (Tübingen: Mohr).

Weber, Max (1924b), 'Socialism', in W. G. Runciman (ed.), *Max Weber: Selections in Translation* (Cambridge: Cambridge University Press, 1978).

Wilson, H. T. (1977), *The American Ideology: Science, Technology and Organisation as Modes of Rationality in Advanced Industrial Societies* (London: Routledge & Kegan Paul).

Wolters, F. (1930), *Stefan George und die Blätter für die Kunst* (Berlin: Bondi).

Index